HELLO DARLING!

THE COMPLETE ENGRAVER

MONOGRAMS, CRESTS, CIPHERS, SEALS, AND THE ETIQUETTE OF SOCIAL STATIONERY

Nancy Sharon Collins

FOREWORD BY ELLEN LUPTON

ESSAY BY MARJORIE B. COHN

PRINCETON ARCHITECTURAL PRESS · NEW YORK

opposite:
Classic contemporary hand-engraved tree by banknote engraver John S. Wallace. The print (3/8 of an inch tall) was made from a half-inch-thick steel die that was given to the author and her late husband on the occasion of the loss of approximately fifty mature trees during Hurricane Katrina.

PUBLISHED BY
PRINCETON ARCHITECTURAL PRESS
37 EAST 7TH STREET
NEW YORK, NEW YORK 10003

VISIT OUR WEBSITE AT WWW.PAPRESS.COM

PRINTED AND BOUND IN CHINA
15 14 13 12 4 3 2 1 FIRST EDITION

EDITORS: SARA BADER AND NICOLA BEDNAREK BROWER
DESIGNERS: PAUL WAGNER AND ELANA SCHLENKER

SPECIAL THANKS TO: BREE ANNE APPERLEY, SARA BADER, JANET BEHNING, FANNIE BUSHIN, MEGAN CAREY, CARINA CHA, ANDREA CHLAD, RUSSELL FERNANDEZ, JAN HAUX, LINDA LEE, DIANE LEVINSON, JENNIFER LIPPERT, JACOB MOORE, GINA MORROW, KATHARINE MYERS, MARGARET ROGALSKI, DAN SIMON, SARA STEMEN, ANDREW STEPANIAN, AND JOSEPH WESTON OF PRINCETON ARCHITECTURAL PRESS
—KEVIN C. LIPPERT, PUBLISHER

LIBRARY OF CONGRESS
CATALOGING-IN-PUBLICATION DATA
COLLINS, NANCY SHARON.
THE COMPLETE ENGRAVER : A GUIDE TO MONOGRAMS, CRESTS, CIPHERS, SEALS, AND THE ETIQUETTE AND HISTORY OF SOCIAL STATIONERY / NANCY SHARON COLLINS. — FIRST EDITION.
PAGES CM
INCLUDES BIBLIOGRAPHICAL REFERENCES AND INDEX.
ISBN 978-1-61689-067-4 (HARDCOVER : ALK. PAPER)
1. ENGRAVING. 2. MONOGRAMS. 3. SOCIAL STATIONERY. I. TITLE.
NE2700.C65 2012
769.5—DC23
2012003848

TO MY LATE HUSBAND

John Mack Collins

Table of Contents

FOREWORD

ELLEN LUPTON

In 1997 Nancy Sharon Collins visited me at the Cooper-Hewitt, National Design Museum in New York City, carrying a folder stocked with luscious specimens of engraving. My tiny office at the time was located, appropriately enough, just off the museum's library—a divinely decrepit vault whose open stacks overflowed with centuries of printed matter, there for the browsing. Nancy had been sent my way by another elegant nerd, Stephen Doyle, who knew I would be as mesmerized as he was by Nancy's curious sheets of hieratic monograms and lacquered alphabets.

The year before I had produced an exhibition called *Letters from the Avant-Garde* (the catalog was published in 1996 by Princeton Architectural Press). The project showed how the legendary modernist movements of the twentieth century had used printed stationery to communicate with a far-flung community of like-minded rebels. Imagine that: a rebel with a letterhead. *Letters from the Avant-Garde* was a collaboration with the legendary artist and collector Elaine Lustig

Cohen, who stored her personal stash of vanguard stationery under a bed in her East Side townhouse. Most of the pieces in Cohen's collection were printed letterpress; in the 1920s and 1930s, engraving was already so last century. Hardworking and commonplace, letterpress suited the constructivist mechanics of El Lissitzky and László Moholy-Nagy.

In our book and exhibition, our sole example of engraving came from the Cooper-Hewitt's extraordinary archive of Ladislav Sutnar. The great Czech modernist had preserved among his papers a pair of before-and-after letterheads from the 1920s. The older, vernacular design had been engraved, featuring slim geometric letters and a delicate line drawing of a factory, arranged in a single banner across the top of the page. Similar factories in similar layouts adorned countless commercial letterheads of the nineteenth and twentieth centuries. For his modernist redo, Sutnar organized the elements in functional zones, following the theory of the New Typography advocated by Jan Tschichold and others. Sutnar used bands of color, type, and image to mark off areas of the page, activating the entire sheet. The factory was still there, redrawn in simple, heavy lines, and the type was set in clunky Futura. The printing method was letterpress.

In the postwar period, offset pushed aside both letterpress and engraving for most corporate identity work. Engraving survived as a marker of luxury and decorum. I experienced the process in person during a private tour of Crane & Co.'s factory in Dalton, Massachusetts, which produces custom social stationery, wedding invitations, executive business papers, and the like. In the factory's engraving area, I watched a skilled operator position each piece by hand on a press that forced the paper against an intaglio surface, creating a raised imprint on the front and a distinctive bruise on the back. That bruise is the medium's badge of honor.

Nancy, who owned and operated a graphic design studio in New York, started to focus on engraving in 1995, opening her own studio, Nancy Sharon Collins, Stationer, now located in Louisiana. There she has lived, worked, and thrived since 2004, and there she mourned the death of her beloved husband, John Mack Collins, in 2010. This book is dedicated to him. He would have liked to share it with his devoted collaborator in the inky matter of print. Today, Nancy brings crisp wit and undying love to one of history's most spirited printing processes. As the letterpress revival grips designers in its leaden thrall, we might ready ourselves to receive engraving's lighter touch.

I've recently succumbed to an obsession of my own. I'm writing a novel, set in the near future, an imagined destiny in which all manner of communication technologies comingle in a mild-mannered utopia. Our young protagonist is an overeducated art school graduate seeking success in New York City. Early in the novel, she is slipped a calling card that beckons with opportunity:

> The raised hairlines of the letterforms—Gotham Rounded Extra Light Reverse Italic (6 pt, all caps)—glistened in the dim incandescence of the nightclub. A blunt depression bruised the card's soft ivory backside. This thick wafer of Mohawk Superfine Ivory Cover stock was no cheap thermographic heat job. It had been engraved, by hand, in a real factory somewhere, a river rushing by. Perhaps this unbearably elegant slice of printed matter was doomed to the same trash heap as the cocktail napkin with which I wiped my fevered brow. But maybe, just maybe, it would lead me to a better life. Was I ready to heed its call?
>
> Yes, I said, yes, I will. Yes.

INTRODUCTION

The history of engraving parallels the evolution of movable type and letterpress printing. As a commercial endeavor, it is integral to the study of graphic design, although to date its influences are usually found in the corners and margins of documented history. When I began discovering references to engraving in important moments throughout design and print history, starting in the mid-fifteenth century with Johannes Gutenberg's now famous movable type, I realized that this is a crucial story to tell.

While Gutenberg, credited by some as being the father of popular media, was busy typesetting and printing his 42-line Bible, he was also trying to develop a cost-efficient means for commercial engraving. Depending upon which version of the story you read, his backers either took advantage of him or he was not a great businessman, because his engraving venture went nowhere. However, investing in the technology of printing imagery and type simultaneously made good business sense. Engraved images at that time were from copperplates, which are thinner than the type-high standard for letterpress. Therefore, to print both text and imagery on the same sheet required two separate set-ups and press runs: one pass through the press for type and a separate pass for the image. The invention of a way to produce illustrations within the confines of a letterpress machine, with its flexibility in easily changing and reusing type, could have been a potential industry breakthrough. It might have altered print and design history forever, shifting our type-heavy historic gaze to a more inclusive print tradition of how words and images were created to fit together. It would take an additional three hundred years, with the advent of lithography, for this synthesis of word and image to occur, and it was later still, with the invention of photo-mechanical processes, that the book publishing industry fully benefited from the simultaneous printing of type and pictures.

Compared to letterpress printing, where individual blocks of type are organized in a grid [**Figs. 1, 2**], engraving is a more fluid, freehand expression restricted only by the shape of the piece of material on which the engraver works. Traditionally, engravings were usually made by cutting into either wood, steel, or copper. [**Figs. 3, 4**] This book primarily focuses on metal engraving, specifically its more prosaic printed forms, such as stationery. Many fine books and articles cover the subject of wood engraving, but metal engraving has become its shy second sister.

In general, wood engraving is an easier method to learn than engraving on the less forgiving surfaces of steel and copper. Although fine wood engraving is difficult to master, wood itself is easier to work with and therefore became a popular means to illustrate newspapers, magazines, and pulp fiction, while steel and copper engraving plates were reserved for more high-end imagery. Indeed, woodcut printing is the oldest printmaking method known. It was first developed in Europe around 1400 BCE, about six centuries after it was established in the East. In this process, all but the areas intended for print are carefully cut from the surface with a sharp tool.[1] When the wood block is inked and an impression made on paper, the result is a relief print. [**Figs. 5–7**]

THE HAMILTON MFG. CO.
California Job Case, $0 90
Most popular of all Job Cases. Note the large cap boxes.
Used exclusively in all our type cabinets
unless otherwise ordered.

Fig. 1, top:
Metal type set by hand in a chase, showing the rigidity of a letterpress lock-up.

Fig. 2, bottom:
In traditional letterpress printing each row of text is composed of individual letters cast on rectangular blocks, allowing for vertical alignment or justification when locked in the chase with spacing material. The grid system imposes a formal organizational structure to typesetting design. The type case shown here is known as a California job case; its compartments are organized so that more frequently used letters and spaces are within convenient reach of the typesetter, thereby speeding up the typesetting process.
American Specimen Book of Type Styles (Jersey City, NJ: American Type Founders Co., 1912), 1,274. Collection of Mark von Bronkhorst, *Albany, California.*

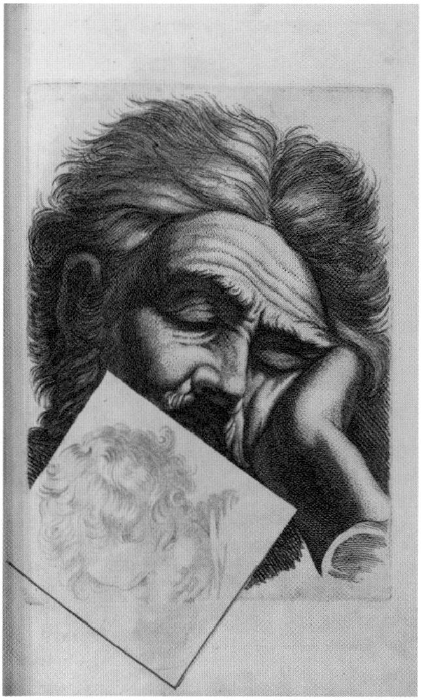

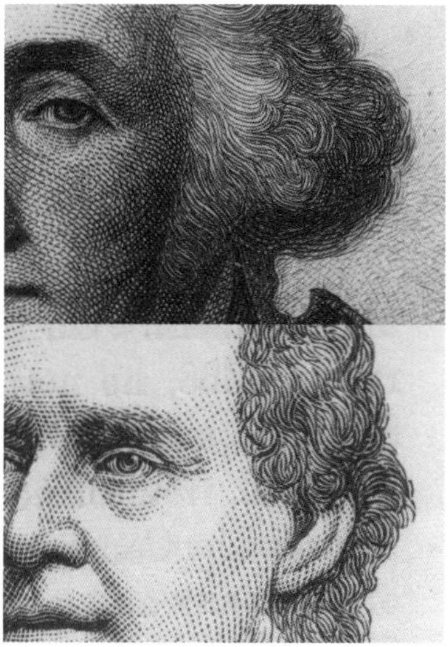

Fig. 3, left:
This example of metal engraving by George Bickham is included in *The Museum of Arts: or, The Curious Repository* (London: George Bickham, ca. 1730), which appears to be a kind of workbook, perhaps for Bickham's famous engraved copy book, *The Universal Penman*. Some pages look as if they were done for the pure pleasure of engraving rather than to illustrate a particular alphabet, lettering style, or text.
Harry Ransom Center, the University of Texas at Austin.

Fig. 4, right:
Two illustrations from the same book, showing a detail of a metal engraving (top) and a detail of a wood engraving (bottom). The difference between the two engraving and printing processes is evident: in the top example, a very sharp, small blade was used to incise the lines, which vary in width at the entrance and exit points; in the bottom example, the lines are the result of material having been cut away from the wood's surface and do not taper but begin and end more abruptly.
John Clark Ridpath, *Cyclopaedia of Universal History* (Cincinnati: Jones Brothers Publishing Co., 1885).

Fig. 5:
The Springer, or Cocker, wood engraving by Thomas Bewick (1753–1828). Bewick, perhaps the most famous wood engraver, is credited with popularizing the use of end-grain specimens of boxwood, a specific species of wood that allowed for greater detail, longevity, and longer press runs. The hard surface of end-grain wood can generate more print impressions than the softer long-grain wood (the long side of a plank of wood), which was traditionally used for woodcut printing. Bewick greatly influenced the development of illustrated book production, because the finer, sharper tools employed in metal engraving could be used on end-grain wood, allowing for minute detail previously achieved only in metal. As with wood block print-ing, wood engraving could be made type high so that pictures and text could be composed and printed together rather than in separate press runs still necessary for metal engravings. The illustrations in figures 5 and 6 were first published by Bewick in his landmark book *A General History of Quadrupeds* (1790).
John Rayner, *A Selection of Engravings on Wood* by Thomas Bewick (London and New York: Penguin Books, 1947).

Fig. 6, opposite, top:
Thomas Bewick, *Newfoundland Dog*.
John Rayner, *A Selection of Engravings on Wood* by Thomas Bewick (London and New York: Penguin Books, 1947).

Fig. 7, opposite, bottom:
Woodblock print by Emily DeLorge, Houma, Louisiana, 2011. This is a contemporary example of relief printing.

B
1789
P·V·B·B

In contrast, engraved metal creates an intaglio print, in which the carved areas make up the image. A very sharp, knifelike blade called a burin, or graver, is used to cut fine lines or dots. When ink is rubbed into the cuts and the surface is wiped clean, the ink stays within the cut channels. A piece of paper is then placed on top and pressure (about two tons per square inch on a commercial press) is applied, forcing the paper into the inked areas. When the paper is pulled away, the transferred ink remains. Because of the extreme pressure used in this process, the ink is raised and can be felt by fingertip, and the backside often features an indentation called a bruise. These are the telltale marks of engraving. [**Figs. 8, 9**]

Thank You

Fig. 8, top:
Bruise on the back of a hand-engraved thank-you card.
Commissioned by the author, New York, 1999.

Fig. 9, bottom:
Front of hand-engraved thank-you card, showing book edge gilding, done by hand, and radiused corners.
Commissioned by the author, New York, 1999.

Engraving is an expedient means of expression. When it is mastered, it is a fairly direct method to make multiple copies of a design, because all that is required is a surface into which you can cut, a tool sharp enough to incise an image, ink, paper, and pressure. Over the centuries engraving has been utilized for book illustration; serial reproduction of popular books and prints (e.g., John James Audubon's edition of 435 full-scale prints in *Birds of America*) [**Fig. 10**]; fine art imagery; portraits of famous people [**Fig. 11**]; governmental, civic, and theological proclamations; political commentary and satire [**Figs. 12, 13**]; cartography [**Fig. 14**]; and fine wine labels; and as a safety feature to prevent forgery [**Fig. 15**] of currency and other instruments of finance, such as stock and bond certificates and postal stamps.

Another important product of engraving is social stationery, which has traditionally been commercially engraved. Engraved imagery can convey a wide range of ideas and emotions. Quick, emotive sketches—thin, light lines in consort with bold, dark, thick, and deep ones—express feeling, stories, and opinion. [**Fig. 16**] This may be an overly simplistic reason for why engraving and etching was, for centuries, used to communicate political irony and social injustice.[2] Think of Francisco de Goya's etchings *Disasters of War*, powerful indictments against the horrors of armed conflict, or nineteenth-century engravings depicting African Americans, indigenous Americans, and politicians in egregious stereotypical roles. [**Fig. 17**] Editions of engraved prints with timely social and political commentary were once common forms of popular entertainment that sold well and brought fast cash to the creator. Printers and print shops would advertise, display, and sell each new installment of, say, a William Hogarth morality series, a Paul Revere[3, 4] print [**Fig. 18**], or bawdy caricatures of the historic event that inspired the coining of the now popular phrase "financial bubble." [**Figs. 19, 20**] So engraving was, in a sense, an early form of blogging: if your storefront became known for retailing prints depicting the hottest scandal, everyone flocked to your site, much like followers of social media today.[5]

Fig. 10, left:
John James Audubon, *Barred Owl*, from *Birds of America* (London: George Bickham, 1827–1838), vol. 1, plate 46. Watercolored engraving with aquatint.
E. A. McIlhenny Natural History Collection, Louisiana State University (LSU) Libraries, Baton Rouge, Louisiana.

Fig. 11, right:
Charles Burt, ca. 1875. Steel engraving of Henry Wadsworth Longfellow.
The Historic New Orleans Collection, accession no. 1993.143.1.

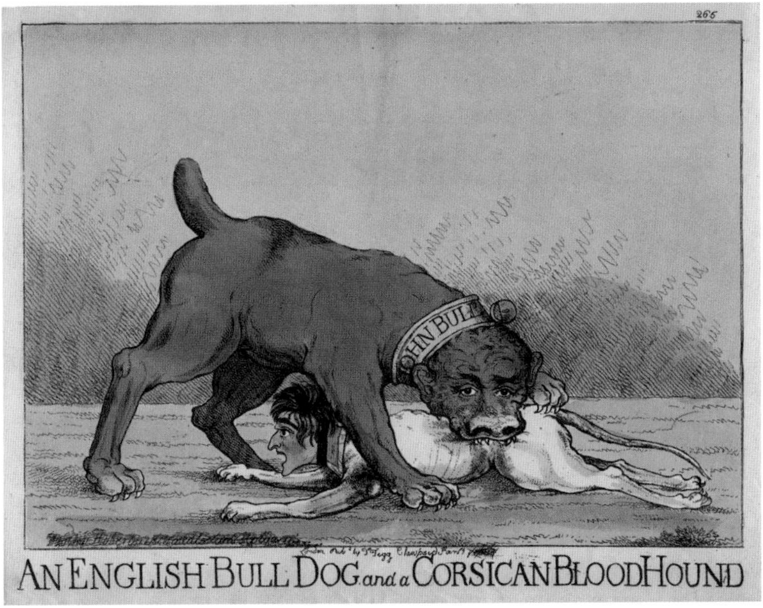
265
JOHN BULL
AN ENGLISH BULL DOG and a CORSICAN BLOOD HOUND

THE CORSICAN SPIDER IN HIS WEB!

Fig. 12, top:
Thomas Tegg, *An English Bull Dog and a Corsican Blood Hound* (London, ca. 1803), etching.
Napoleonic Satires collection, Anne S. K. Brown Military Collection, Brown University Library.

Fig. 13, bottom:
Thomas Rowlandson, *The Corsican Spider in His Web!* (London, 1808), etching.
Anne S. K. Brown Military Collection.

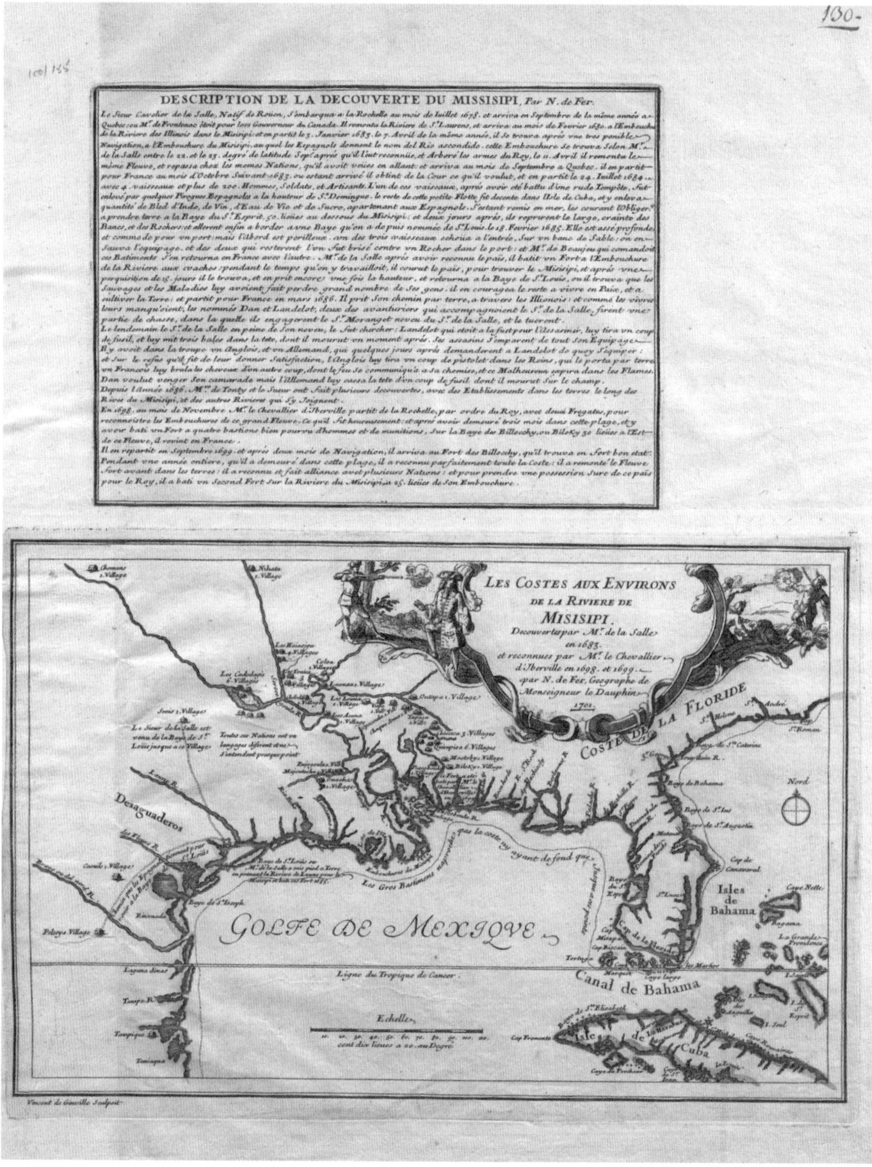
DESCRIPTION DE LA DECOUVERTE DU MISSISIPI, Par N. de Fer.
Les Costes aux Environs de la Riviere de Misisipi. Decouvertes par Mr. de la Salle en 1683. et reconnues par Mr. le Chevallier d'Iberville en 1698. et 1699. par N. de Fer, Geographe de Monseigneur le Dauphin. 1701.
Coste de la Floride
Golfe de Mexique
Desaguaderos
Canal de Bahama
Isles de Bahama
Isle de Cuba
Ligne du Tropique de Cancer.
Echelle
Nord
Vincent de Gouville Sculpsit

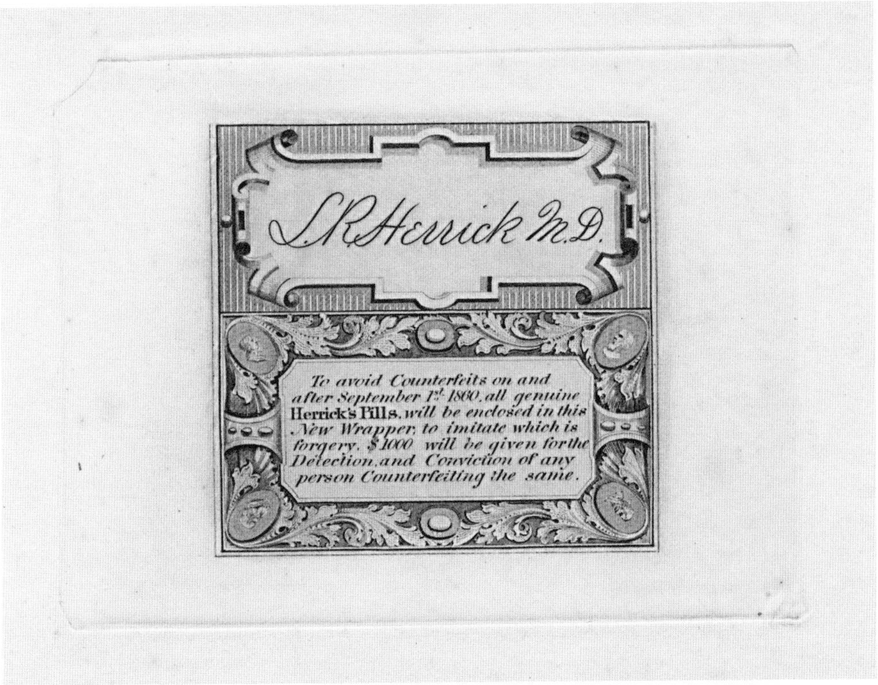
S.R. Herrick M.D.
To avoid Counterfeits on and
after September 1st 1860, all genuine
Herrick's Pills, will be enclosed in this
New Wrapper, to imitate which is
forgery. $1000 will be given for the
Detection, and Conviction of any
person Counterfeiting the same.

Fig. 14, opposite:
Nicholas de Fer, *Costes aux environs de la Riviere de Misisipi* (1701), early engraved map of the state of Louisiana. It is possible to see the impressions made by the copperplates around the perimeter of each of the two images.
Louisiana and Lower Mississippi Valley Collections, LSU Libraries.

Fig. 15, top:
Press proof of Herrick's Pills wrapper, engraved to prevent counterfeiting (1860).
Collection of Richard D. Sheaff.

Fig. 16, right:
This detail of a hand-engraved cipher for a valentine card illustrates the delicate curves and very thin lines that can be achieved through engraving. It also exhibits what is called an orange peel effect, a bumpy surface that results from open cuts, or large areas of ink coverage without screening, mezzotint, hatching, or cross-hatching. Viewed at full size this texture is almost unnoticeable.
Engraved by Tommy Flax, New York, commissioned by Jeffery R. McKay, Miami, 2006.

The PRAIRIE DOG sickened at the sting of the HORNET
or a Diplomatic Puppet exhibiting his Deceptions!

Fig. 17, top:
James Akin, *The Prairie Dog Sickened at the Sting of the Hornet or a Diplomatic Puppet Exhibiting His Deceptions* (Newport, Massachusetts, 1804), etching with watercolor.
Library of Congress Prints and Photographs Division (LC-DIG-ppmsca-01659).

Fig. 18, bottom:
Paul Revere, *The Bloody Massacre Perpetrated in King Street Boston on March 5th 1770 by a Party of the 29th Regt.* (Boston, 1770), engraving.
Library of Congress Prints and Photographs Division (LC-DIG-ppmsca-01657).

Fig. 19:
Frans De Bruyn, *Het Groote Tafereel der Dwaasheid* (The Great Mirror of Folly) (Amsterdam?, 1720?), close-up of "Harlequin stockholder." This satirical engraving was published in *Het Groote Tafereel der Dwaasheid*, which is rather notorious in business management and financial circles, as it is presumed to have first been published within months of the international economic crashes of 1720 involving England, France, and the Dutch Provinces. These speculative crashes began independently and at different times but "burst" almost simultaneously, sending independent investors, stock markets, and some governments into bankruptcy. The book contains page after page of engraved comic depictions of grotesque investing folly.
The Historic New Orleans Collection, accession no. 60–63.

ARLEQUYN ACTIONIST

Fig. 20:
Frans De Bruyn, *Harlequin stockholder* (detail) (Amsterdam?, 1720?), from *Het Groote Tafereel der Dwaasheid.*
The Historic New Orleans Collection, accession no. 60–63.

Despite its once widespread use and appeal, engraving remains a little-studied field in graphic design. Letterpress is the undeniable structure and basis for how we, as a Western design culture, have learned to see and organize our visual world. Some of the best examples of engraving are considered art, not graphic design. For many, it remains the highest form of print, its beauty appreciated by almost anyone who has the opportunity to experience its romantically expressive lines. Engraving's golden arches (those wild, irreverent loops and curls that define real steel- or copperplate engraving), delicate hatching and crosshatching, and contouring and cross-contouring [**Figs. 21, 22**] are typically discussed in art history class, where students are introduced to examples of engraved fine art prints, usually in the context of reproductions of masterpiece paintings, designs on precious metals and gems, and decorative arts.

In the graphic design classroom today, smaller movements such as engraving are overshadowed by trends and processes with more direct contemporary relevance. Part of the reason for this is that only a small portion of typographic history can be directly linked to metal engraving. There are other reasons as well. For centuries engraving was considered the domain of scholars, princes, and kings, those who highly valued aesthetics and the finer details of the visual world. Because traditional forms of fine art engraving were very expensive to produce, the practice and process has long maintained a mystique and has been deemed a higher, exclusive form of print. Passing on the skill of engraving was not a simple task, either. An apprenticeship to a master engraver required a serious commitment of time and, more importantly, a great deal of aptitude. Engraving was reserved for those with obvious artistic talents, stunningly accurate eyesight, superb hand–eye coordination, and fine motor skills. For all these reasons mainstream media gravitated to and adopted more accessible and adaptable modes of print production, such as letterpress, lithography, and, later, digital printing.

With some exceptions, the commercial engraving process has not significantly changed in a century.[6] Unfortunately, craftsmen working

Fig. 21, top:
In engraving, the effect of shading is achieved by subtle variations of line width and spacing. The play from thick to thin lines, contouring and cross-contouring, suggests, when viewed at a normal reading distance, rich tonal variations as well as form and mass. This detail of a banknote engraving of Martha Washington illustrates figurative shading and modeling with the use of cross-contour.

Fig. 22, bottom:
Banknote engraving of Martha Washington (cropped), matted and mounted on board with decorative cord for hanging. This engraving was a promotional Christmas gift distributed by Standard Ink & Color Company (Brooklyn, New York, ca. 1920).
Collection of Hart Engraving, Milwaukee.

today are few and often underappreciated. Fifty years ago, there were nearly a thousand presses printing commercial engraving in this country. Today, fewer than a third of these exist. The commercial engravers' trade organization membership peaked in the 1980s with approximately 140 members but has since dropped to forty-four. When these businesses close, presses, engraving machines, and thousands of beautiful plates and dies head to the junkyard for scrap. This is a huge and untimely loss. Just as neighborhood stationers and local engravers are shutting their doors, more and more young people are becoming curious about the craft and process. In an increasingly "high-tech but low-touch" world, students and design practitioners want to experience how print is made. This book aims to share the history and practice of engraving, to encourage readers to view graphic design and type through the lens of this exquisite, if lofty, commercial art.

Engraved stationery, and in particular social stationery, is especially interesting in this regard, as it serves as a medium for communication between a sender and a recipient. Our emotional response to these pieces of engraved papers is deeper than that to other examples of engraving, such as stocks, bonds, or wine labels. Moreover, engraved stationery provides not only a striking opportunity to study the art of commercial engraving but also introduces us to some of the cultural traditions involved in the writing of a letter or a note.

A TIMELINE OF ENGRAVING

Because engraving once touched so many aspects of our lives, the following timeline includes references to fine art printmaking, typography, cartography, philately, print history and the book arts, industrial history, graphic design, literature, and popular culture.

MID-1400S
AN ENGRAVER KNOWN BY THE MONIKER "MASTER OF THE PLAYING CARDS" IS GENERALLY RECOGNIZED AS THE FIRST MASTER COPPERPLATE ENGRAVER. HIS WORK INCLUDED MOTIFS (SUCH AS BIRDS OF DIFFERENT SHAPES AND PLUMAGE) ASSUMED TO HAVE BEEN CREATED TO MAKE PLAYING CARDS, A COMMON FORM OF ENTERTAINMENT.

MID-1400S
JOHANNES GUTENBERG (CA. 1398–1468), WHILE DEVELOPING SYSTEMS THAT MADE MOVABLE TYPE POSSIBLE, ALSO TRIES TO INVENT A COMMERCIALLY VIABLE METHOD OF MAKING COPPERPLATE ENGRAVING COMPATIBLE WITH LETTER-PRESS PRINTING.[1] IF SUCCESSFUL, GUTENBERG WOULD HAVE SIGNIFICANTLY REDUCEDTHE TIME, EFFORT, AND PRODUCTION COSTS OF BOOK PUBLISHING.

1400S
HUMANISTIC (OR HUMANIST) STYLE IN TYPOGRAPHY EMERGES IN ITALY. THE PARTNERSHIP OF KONRAD SWEYNHEIM (?–1476) AND ARNOLD PANNARTZ (?–1477), BOTH PRINTERS AND THE FIRST IN ITALY TO PRINT BOOKS USING MOVABLE TYPE, IS CENTRAL TO THE EVOLUTION FROM BLACK LETTER, IN WHICH GUTENBERG'S BIBLE WAS SET, TO OLD STYLE.[2] SWEYNHEIM, WHO WAS ORIGINALLY AN ENGRAVER, AND PANNARTZ WORKED TOGETHER FOR SEVERAL YEARS, CREATING A NEW STYLE OF TYPE THAT WAS INFLUENCED BY CALLIGRAPHY PREVALENT IN ITALY AT THAT TIME.

LATE 1400S
MASTER DRAFTSMAN MARTIN SCHONGAUER (CA. 1448–1491) IS CONSIDERED ONE OF THE MOST, IF NOT THE MOST, IMPORTANT GERMAN ENGRAVERS BEFORE ALBRECHT DÜRER.

LATE 1400s–EARLY 1500s
THE ENGRAVINGS, WOODCUTS, AND ETCHINGS OF MASTER DRAFTSMAN ALBRECHT DÜRER (1471–1528), A GODSON OF A VERY SUCCESSFUL GERMAN PRINTER AND PUBLISHER, ARE CONSIDERED AMONG THE MOST IMPORTANT EXAMPLES OF THESE PROCESSES. HE WAS ALSO A PAINTER AND A THEORIST OF MATHEMATICS, PERSPECTIVE, REPRESENTATION, THE PHILOSOPHIC IDEAL, AND CLASSICAL PROPORTIONS IN ART. [**Fig. 1**]

EARLY 1500s
GEOFFROY TORY (CA. 1480–1533), A FRENCH PUBLISHER, PRINTER, AND ENGRAVER, CHAMPIONS THE NEW HUMANIST TYPE IN FRANCE AND MENTORS CLAUDE GARAMOND (CA. 1490–1561), WHO BECAME A LEADING TYPE DESIGNER.

Fig. 1:
Contemporary commercially engraved die based on the mark with which Dürer signed much of his work.
Commissioned by the author, Covington, Louisiana, 2011.

EARLY 1500s
MARCANTONIO RAIMONDI (CA. 1480–CA. 1534), COMMONLY REFERRED TO BY HIS FIRST NAME, IS THE FIRST TO USE ENGRAVING PURELY FOR ITS REPRODUCTIVE QUALITIES. PRIOR TO MARCANTONIO, MOST ENGRAVERS WERE *PEINTER-GRAVEURS*, ARTISTS WHO CREATED THEIR OWN ORIGINAL WORKS RATHER THAN COPYING A PAINTING OR DRAWING BY ANOTHER ARTIST. MARCANTONIO STRUCK UP A RELATIONSHIP WITH THE DRAWING AND PAINTING MASTER RAPHAEL (1483–1520) AND MADE A HAPPY CAREER OF REPRODUCING THE ARTIST'S WORK IN ENGRAVINGS AND ETCHINGS. THEIR COLLABORATION WAS PERHAPS THE FIRST TO EXPLOIT THIS MARKETING POTENTIAL, SELLING IN QUANTITIES LUCRATIVE TO BOTH ARTISTS.

1600S

LATE 1600S–EARLY 1700S

WRITING MASTERS GEORGE SHELLEY (CA. 1666–1736) AND CHARLES SNELL (1670–1733) BOTH CREATE CALLIGRAPHIC STYLES USED IN TYPOGRAPHY TO THIS DAY. [**Fig. 2**]

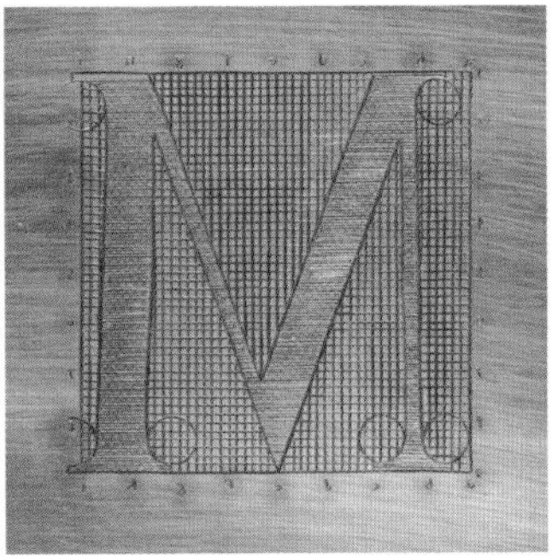

Fig. 3:
Contemporary copperplate engraving exercise of the letter *M* in the style of Romain du Roi. The line work is not as refined as that of the 1692 original, as it was made by a beginning engraver.
Engraved by Emily DeLorge, Houma, Louisiana, 2011.

Fig. 2:
Example of calligraphic engraving from George Shelley, *Natural Writing in All the Hands: With Variety of Ornament* (London: Bowles?, between 1764 and 1779), a copy book engraved by George Bickham.
TypW 705.64.786, plate 5, Houghton Library, Harvard University.

1702

THE TYPEFACE ROMAIN DU ROI IS CREATED IN FRANCE [**Fig. 3**] IN RESPONSE TO KING LOUIS XIV'S FORMATION OF A COMMITTEE, IN 1692, TO ACHIEVE "A FORMAL PERFECTION IN TYPE DESIGN." LOUIS SIMONNEAU (1654–1727) ENGRAVED THE DESIGNS FOR THE LETTERFORMS IN PRECISE, GEOMETRIC CONFORMITY TO SHOW "MATHEMATICAL PERFECTION." THIS WAS A DRAMATIC DEPARTURE FROM THE HUMANIST STYLE PRECEDING IT. THE TYPEFACE ITSELF WAS CUT BY PHILIPPE GRANDJEAN (1666–1714). INTENTIONALLY OR NOT, HE TOOK ARTISTIC LICENSE INTERPRETING THE ORIGINAL ENGRAVINGS, SOFTENING THEIR UNAPPROACHABLE, GEOMETRIC RIGIDITY.

1700s

1743
GEORGE BICKHAM THE ELDER (CA. 1684–1758), ENGLISH WRITING MASTER AND CALLIGRAPHIC ENGRAVER, PUBLISHES *THE UNIVERSAL PENMAN*, WHICH INCLUDES THE WORK OF SHELLEY AND SNELL AND IS STILL IN PRINT TODAY.

EARLY TO MID-1700s
WILLIAM CASLON (1692–1766), WHO RECEIVED HIS EARLY TRAINING AS AN ENGRAVER OF GUN BARRELS, ESTABLISHES HIS INFLUENTIAL TYPE FOUNDRY, IN LONDON.

1792
STEEL ENGRAVING DEVELOPED IN AMERICA BY JACOB PERKINS (1766–1849) FOR THE PRINTING OF NONFORGEABLE BANKNOTES. THE PROCESS IS ALSO DEVELOPED IN ENGLAND IN THE 1820S AS AN ALTERNATIVE TO COPPERPLATE PRINTING; FINER LINES COULD BE INCISED ON THE HARDER METAL, AND ITS GREATER DURABILITY ENABLED MANY MORE IMPRESSIONS TO BE MADE FROM ONE PLATE OR DIE.

1798
GERMAN ACTOR AND PLAYWRIGHT ALOIS SENEFELDER (1771–1834) DEVELOPS COMMERCIAL LITHOGRAPHY, A MAJOR TECHNOLOGICAL ADVANCEMENT, AND PATENTS IT ONE YEAR LATER. WITH THIS PROCESS TEXT AND IMAGE COULD BE PRINTED SIMULTANEOUSLY, WHICH HALVED THE RESOURCES REQUIRED AND OPENED UP NEW ARTISTIC FREEDOM TO EARLY ADOPTERS AND GENERATIONS OF LITHOGRAPHIC PRINTERS.

LATE 1700s–EARLY 1800s
ENGLISHMAN THOMAS BEWICK (1753–1828), TRAINED AS A METAL ENGRAVER, PIONEERS THE WHITE-LINE METHOD OF WOOD ENGRAVING.

1800s

1807

THE CAMERA LUCIDA IS PATENTED BY WILLIAM HYDE WALLASTON (1766–1828). [**Fig. 4**] THE DRAWING AID CONTAINS A LENS THAT OPTICALLY SUPERIMPOSES AN IMAGE ONTO A DRAWING SURFACE, ENABLING AN ARTIST TO TRACE THE PROJECTION.

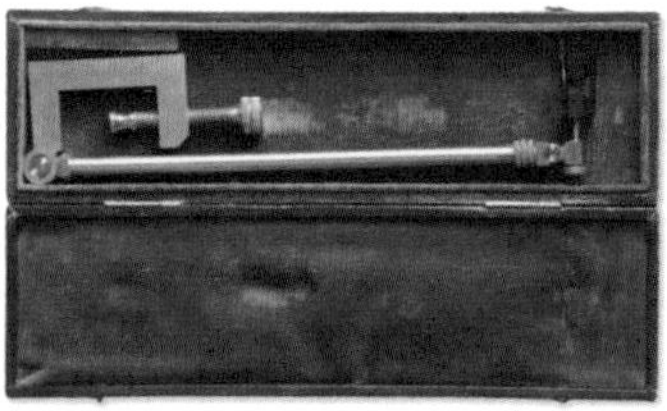

Fig. 4:
Camera lucida.

1826

THE FIRST KNOWN PHOTOGRAPH, BY NICÉPHORE NIÉPCE (1765–1833), IS CAPTURED WITH THE USE OF A CAMERA OBSCURA.

1827–28

JOHN JAMES AUDUBON (1785–1851), SELF-TAUGHT ORNITHOLOGIST, NATURALIST, AND PAINTER, PUBLISHES THE WILDLY POPULAR *BIRDS OF AMERICA*, WHICH WAS SOLD BY SUBSCRIPTION TO WEALTHY NEW WORLD ENTHUSIASTS IN GREAT BRITAIN. THE FIRST EDITION WAS EXTENSIVELY ILLUSTRATED WITH ORIGINAL ENGRAVINGS, ETCHINGS, AND AQUATINTS. [**Fig. 5**]

Fig. 5:
Detail of the squirrel in Audubon's *Barred Owl*, from *Birds of America* (London, 1821), showing some of the intaglio techniques used in the print, specifically aquatint to imply tone and shading. The watercolor was applied by hand.
E. A. McIlhenny Natural History Collection, LSU Libraries.

1800s

POSTAGE
A ONE PENNY. I

Fig. 6:
Engraved Penny Black stamp.

1840
THE PENNY BLACK STAMP IS ISSUED IN BRITAIN, THE FIRST PREPAID POSTAL STAMP IN THE WORLD. [**Fig. 6**] PREVIOUSLY, POSTAGE WAS PAID BY THE RECIPIENT. THE ENGRAVING ON THE STAMP IS A CAMEO PROFILE SET AGAINST A GUILLOCHE, A PATTERN CREATED BY REPEATING A SHAPE GENERATED BY A METAL LATHE, ALSO USED AS BORDERING MOTIFS IN CURRENCY AND OTHER INSTRUMENTS OF FINANCE.

1844
PRODUCTION OF THE *NARRATIVE OF THE UNITED STATES EXPLORING EXPEDITION* COMMENCES. THIS AMBITIOUS PUBLICATION (FIVE VOLUMES, 2,500 PAGES, 350 ILLUSTRATIONS) EMPLOYED FIFTY ENGRAVERS AND ENGRAVING COMPANIES.

1847
THE FIRST ENGRAVED U.S. POSTAL STAMP IS ISSUED.

1856
THE BESSEMER PROCESS FOR CONVERTING IRON INTO STEEL IS INTRODUCED IN ENGLAND, MAKING THE MATERIAL WIDELY ACCESSIBLE FOR STEEL ENGRAVING.

1800s

MID-1800s–EARLY 1900s
THE HEYDAY OF STEEL ENGRAVING (ALSO CALLED LINE ENGRAVING) FOR THE REPRODUCTION OF ILLUSTRATIVE WORK IN MASS MEDIA.

1862
THE FIRST AMERICAN PAPER CURRENCY IS ENGRAVED AND PRINTED AT THE TREASURY DEPARTMENT.
[**Figs. 7, 8**]

1896
THE NATIONAL ASSOCIATION OF PHOTO-ENGRAVERS IS FOUNDED, WITH SIXTY-SEVEN MEMBERS.

LATE 1800s–EARLY 1900s
THE HOBBY OF CIPHER, MONOGRAM, FAMILY CREST, AND SEAL COLLECTING BECOMES A FAD.

Continental
BANK NOTE Co.
JOHN A. LOWELL & CO.
NEW ENGLAND AGENTS.
NEW YORK
TREMONT STREET.
COR. BOYLSTON.
BOSTON.

Fig. 7:
A fine example of banknote engraving. John A. Lowell & Co., Boston, sometime before 1887.
Collection of Richard D. Sheaff.

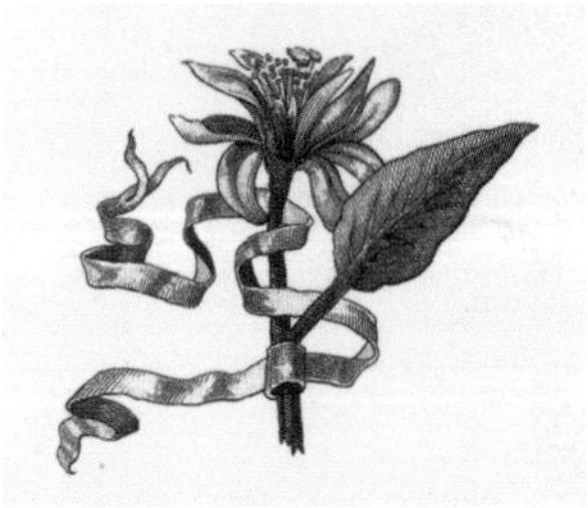

Fig. 8:
Botanical engraving in the banknote style by John Wallace, who, from the late 1940s to the 1990s, worked for most of the banknote engraving companies in the United States, including the Bureau of Engraving and Printing, a bureau within the U.S. Department of Treasury.

1900s

1911
THE *ENCYCLOPEDIA BRITANNICA* IS ILLUSTRATED ENTIRELY WITH STEEL ENGRAVINGS.

1914–18
World War I

1929
THE START OF THE GREAT DEPRESSION, THE PERIOD IN WHICH SOME STATIONERY ENGRAVERS WERE ABLE TO ESTABLISH SUCCESSFUL BUSINESSES OR SURVIVE BY CATERING TO SPECIFIC MARKETS. ECONOMIC RECESSIONS OFTEN INSPIRE ORDINARY WORKERS TO BECOME ENTREPRENEURS. THE MATERIALS AND EQUIP-MENT NECESSARY FOR ENGRAVING WERE RELATIVELY ACCESSIBLE AND GOOD INVESTMENTS. [**Fig. 9**]

1939–45
World War II

1941
PHOTOENGRAVERS RESEARCH INSTITUTE (PERI) IS FORMED. PERI AND THE INTERNATIONAL PHOTOPLATEMAKERS ASSOCIATION BECOME AFFILIATED.

1953
THE CRONITE COMPANY, NEW YORK, IMPLEMENTS AN AUTOMATIC FEEDER ON ENGRAVING PRESSES. PREVIOUSLY, SHEETS OF PAPER, CARDS, AND ENVELOPES WERE HAND FED.

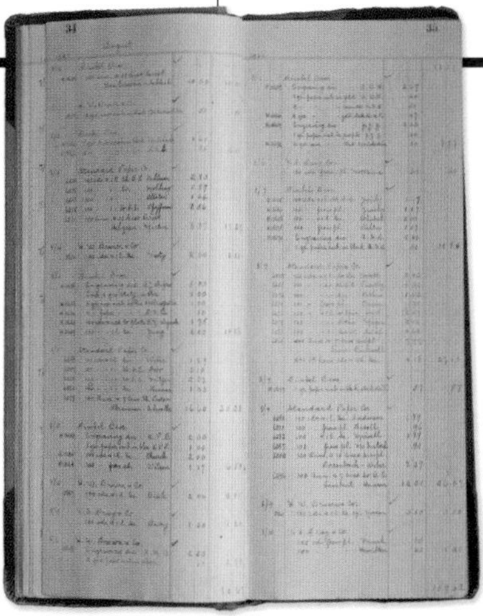

Fig. 9:
1920 accounting ledger from Hart Engraving, Milwaukee, Wisconsin. During the Depression, Mrs. Hart went door-to-door selling her firm's engraving services to well-heeled members of Milwaukee society.
Collection of Hart Engraving, Milwaukee.

1900s

1956–57

DEVELOPMENT OF ESMA-DRY ENGRAVING INK BY THE CAPITOL PRINTING INK COMPANY, WASHINGTON, DC, IN CONJUNCTION WITH THE ENGRAVED STATIONERY MANUFACTURERS RESEARCH INSTITUTE. [**Fig. 10**] IT IS UNCLEAR IF THIS IS THE FIRST ATTEMPT TO CREATE WATER-BASED ENGRAVING INKS, BUT IT WAS THE RESULT OF AN EFFORT TO SHORTEN INK DRYING TIME.

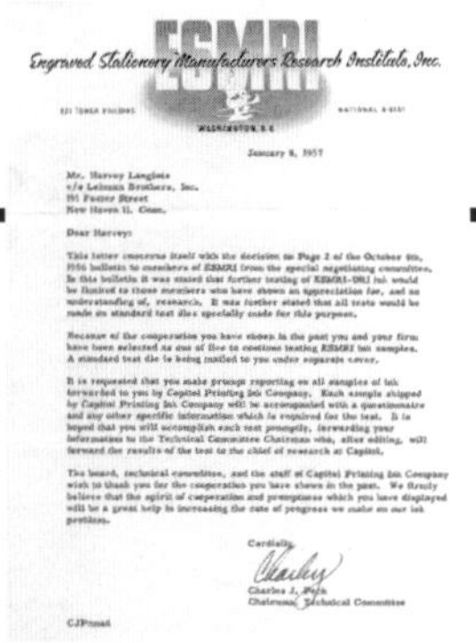

ESMRI
Engraved Stationery Manufacturers Research Institute, Inc.
WASHINGTON, D.C.

January 8, 1957

Mr. Harvey Langlois
c/o Lehmann Brothers, Inc.
[illegible] Foster Street
New Haven 11, Conn.

Dear Harvey:

This letter concerns itself with the decision on Page 2 of the October 4th, 1956 bulletin to members of ESMRI from the special negotiating committee. In this bulletin it was stated that further testing of ESMRI-DRI ink would be limited to those members who have shown an appreciation for, and an understanding of, research. It was further stated that all tests would be made on standard test dies specially made for this purpose.

Because of the cooperation you have shown in the past you and your firm have been selected as one of five to continue testing ESMRI ink samples. A standard test die is being mailed to you under separate cover.

It is requested that you make prompt reporting on all samples of ink forwarded to you by Capitol Printing Ink Company. Each sample shipped by Capitol Printing Ink Company will be accompanied with a questionnaire and any other specific information which is required for the test. It is hoped that you will accomplish each test promptly, forwarding your information to the Technical Committee Chairman who, after editing, will forward the results of the test to the chief of research at Capitol.

The board, technical committee, and the staff of Capitol Printing Ink Company wish to thank you for the cooperation you have shown in the past. We firmly believe that the spirit of cooperation and promptness which you have displayed will be a great help in increasing the rate of progress we make on our ink problem.

Cordially,

Charles J. [illegible]
Chairman, Technical Committee

CJP:[illegible]

Fig. 10:
Letter discussing research on faster-drying commercial engraving ink. The letterhead is engraved in fluorescent pink ink, with a graduating halftone in the background and blind-embossing.

1966

ROBERT N. STEFFENS DEVELOPS AND MARKETS NEW, FAST-DRYING WATER INK, PUSHING OTHER MANUFACTURERS TO MAKE COMPETITIVE PRODUCTS. NINETY-NINE PERCENT OF THE ENGRAVING INK USED IN AMERICA TODAY IS LOW- OR NO-VOC, WATER-BASED INK. [**Fig. 11**]

Standard
Ink & Color Company
Manufacturers of Plate - Printing and Embossing
Inks
Neutral Blue Gloss

Fig. 11:
Page from a varnish-based intaglio ink catalog. This company began developing water-based inks in the 1970s.

1965

A PNEUMATIC SYSTEM OF ENGRAVING POWER TOOLS IS DEVELOPED BY DONALD A. GLASER. IN 1977 GLASER ESTABLISHES THE GLENDO CORPORATION IN EMPORIA, KANSAS, AND IN 2006 EMPORIA STATE UNIVERSITY ANNOUNCES A DEGREE-GRANTING PROGRAM IN ENGRAVING. LEARNING ENGRAVING WITH THIS SYSTEM (ORIGINALLY DEVELOPED FOR COMMERCIAL ENGRAVING) IS MUCH EASIER AND TAKES MUCH LESS TIME THAN TRADITIONAL ENGRAVING.

Early 1960s

POWDERLESS ETCHING FOR COPPER IS DEVELOPED.

1900s

1970s

COMMERCIAL ENGRAVING COMPANIES EXPAND, UTILIZING NEW SALES, MARKETING, AND CUSTOMER SERVICE TECHNIQUES PREVIOUSLY UNCHARACTERISTIC OF THE TRADE. FOR EXAMPLE, WHEN JOE FONTANA AND PARTNERS PURCHASED CHICAGO'S FINE ARTS ENGRAVING COMPANY, IN 1972, ENGRAVING AS THE PREFERRED PRINT TECHNOLOGY FOR CORPORATE IDENTITY SYSTEMS WAS AGGRESSIVELY PROMOTED TO GRAPHIC DESIGNERS AND DESIGN STUDENTS. [**Figs. 12,13**]

1971–80

PERI MERGES WITH THE INTERNATIONAL PHOTOPLATEMAKERS ASSOCIATION (IPA).

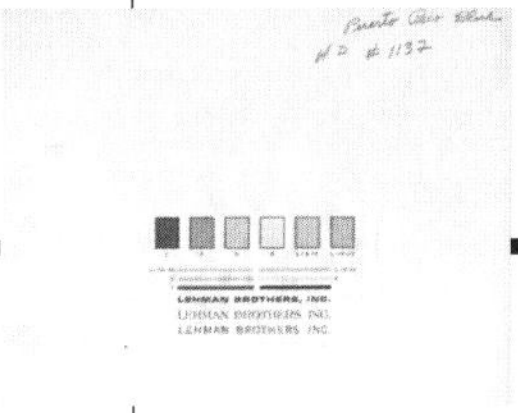

Puerto Rico Rum Institute

1977

THE BATES V. STATE BAR OF ARIZONA SUPREME COURT RULING, WHICH ALLOWED, FOR THE FIRST TIME, LAWYERS TO ADVERTISE THEIR SERVICES, SIGNALS THE TREND AWAY FROM ENGRAVED LEGAL LETTERHEADS. PREVIOUSLY, ALMOST ALL LETTERHEADS USED BY THE LEARNED PROFESSIONS WERE COMMERCIALLY ENGRAVED.

Fig. 12:
Color standard (with varnish-based ink) for the Puerto Rico Rum Institute, New York, ca. 1960s or 1970s.

Fig. 13:
Letterhead for the Puerto Rico Rum Institute, engraved in ink from the color standard illustrated above, ca. 1960s or 1970s.

1900s

1984–85
THE CRONITE COMPANY, NOW IN PARSIPPANY, NEW JERSEY, IMPLEMENTS SHORT-STROKE DESIGN IN THEIR PRESSES, QUADRUPLING THE NUMBER OF IMPRESSIONS POSSIBLE IN THE 1950S AND 1960S.

1985
THE DESKTOP PUBLISHING REVOLUTION IS ENABLED BY APPLE'S MACINTOSH PERSONAL COMPUTER, ITS MACPUBLISHER PAGE LAYOUT SOFTWARE, AND ITS LASERWRITER PRINTER, ALONG WITH ALDUS'S PAGEMAKER SOFTWARE. BY THE EARLY 1990S DIGITAL MEDIA IS WIDELY ADOPTED, MAKING VARIOUS PRINT INDUSTRIES ALMOST OBSOLETE, INCLUDING BUT NOT LIMITED TO TYPESETTING, FILM-AND-PHOTO-RETOUCHING, ANALOG COMMERCIAL PHOTOGRAPHY, OFFSET PLATE ENGRAVING, AND COMMERCIAL STATIONERY ENGRAVING. IRONICALLY, IN THE SAME YEAR, THE ENGRAVED STATIONERY MANUFACTURERS ASSOCIATION BROUGHT TOGETHER GRAPHIC DESIGNERS AND ENGRAVERS IN NEW YORK CITY FOR THE DESIGNER ENGRAVER EXCHANGE, THE FIRST SEMINAR OF ITS KIND.

1990
PORTENTS OF THE DECLINE OF COMMERCIAL ENGRAVING ARE IN EVIDENCE: THE CRONITE COMPANY, FOR EXAMPLE, WAS TAKING ORDERS FOR APPROXIMATELY EIGHTEEN NEW PRESSES PER YEAR PRIOR TO THE 1990S, WHEN THIS NUMBER PRECIPITOUSLY DROPPED TO SIX. TODAY THE FIRM GETS PERHAPS ONE OR TWO ORDERS PER YEAR.

1994–2003
A WASHINGTON, DC, BRAND DESIGN FIRM'S SURVEYS REVEAL A NATIONAL TREND AWAY FROM ENGRAVED LEGAL LETTERHEAD, WHICH HAD BEEN SET IN A UNIFORM STYLE WITH LIMITED VARIETY SINCE THE NINETEENTH CENTURY; THIS DECLINE IN A SIGNIFICANT MARKETPLACE CONTRIBUTES TO THE OVERALL DECLINE OF THE ENGRAVED PRINT INDUSTRY.[3]

CA. 2003–5
CRAFTIVISM, OR CRAFTING FOR A CAUSE, BECOMES AN ESTABLISHED TREND.

2000s

2005
ETSY, AN ONLINE MARKETPLACE FOR HANDMADE AND VINTAGE WARES, LAUNCHES AND QUICKLY ACHIEVES GREAT POPULARITY AND SUCCESS.

2008
LEHMAN BROTHERS INC., A SPECIALTY PRINTING AND ENGRAVING COMPANY, CLOSES AFTER ALMOST A CENTURY IN NEW HAVEN, CONNECTICUT.

2010
BURDGE, INC., AND STUART F. COOPER COMPANY MERGE, FORMING BURDGECOOPER, "THE WORLD'S LARGEST ENGRAVING COMPANY."[4]

THE LOUISIANA ENGRAVERS SOCIETY IS FORMED, HERALDING THE GROWTH OF A PRINT ENGRAVING COMMUNITY IN SOUTH LOUISIANA.

2011
MARK VAN BRONKHORST OF MVB FONTS LAUNCHES THE ROBUST FONT FAMILY SWEET SANS, BASED ON ENGRAVERS' SANS SERIF AND CRONITE MASTERPLATE (SEE APPENDIX A) LINE BLOCK STYLES.

THE COMMERCIAL ENGRAVING INDUSTRY CONTINUES TO CONSOLIDATE: FOR EXAMPLE, DICKSON'S, INC., A SPECIALTY PRINTING AND ENGRAVING COMPANY IN ATLANTA SINCE 1925, CLOSES AND JOINS PRECISE CONTINENTAL, HARRISON, NEW JERSEY, WHICH HAD PREVIOUSLY ACQUIRED REGEN ENGRAVING COMPANY, COLONIAL ENGRAVING COMPANY, BALL ENGRAVING, LYNBROOK ENGRAVING, AND CONTINENTAL CORPORATE ENGRAVERS.

Chapter One

ENGRAVING AND SOCIAL STATIONERY

From the early to mid-1400s, when engraving was first used to create multiple printed copies of a design, the technique was employed to entertain, tell a story, and represent religious thought.[1] Over time, engraving was used to demonstrate artistic virtuosity; create reproductions of original art; illustrate science, math, and technology; and map continents known or newly discovered. In the sixteenth to nineteenth centuries, a small but brilliant movement arose in which gifted writing masters produced prints and specimens of lettering with the tools and devices of engraving, calligraphic in nature and unsurpassed in beauty, for the instruction of proper penmanship, proportion, drawing, and literary ruminations on culture. [**Figs. 1–4**] These so-called copy books, or writing manuals, are fantastically decorative and minutely controlled, with great swoops and long, arching but delicate loops demonstrating alphabets, flourishes, and inspirational sentences. Calligraphic engraving was not for the faint of heart: it required absolute command of both engraving and calligraphy. The profession appealed to neither the masses nor the printmaking community, however, and thus did not thrive.

In the nineteenth century, the proliferation of mass media in the form of newspapers, periodicals, advertisements, and cheap books provided a huge demand for commercially prepared imagery. At the beginning of that century, wood or metal engraving were virtually the only methods commercially available for printing pictures, so master, journeymen, and apprentice engravers were kept busy. Steel and copperplate engravings were used on fiscal instruments [**Fig. 5**] and in high-end books, while woodcut engravings were utilized by newspapers and magazines to illustrate popular culture and the breaking news of the day. At the same time, as great advancements emerged in the manufacture, production, marketing, and sales of virtually everything imaginable (from new corsets to hair products, vacation packages, and never-before-seen electrical appliances), advertising evolved into a trade and discipline of its own, providing ample opportunity for engravers. The heyday for commercial steel and copperplate engraving in the United States lasted

ABC
IKL
RSTU
No. 1.
F K I
H G
A B
D C E
C
No. 4.
O
Q
A P B
I. Merken. fe.

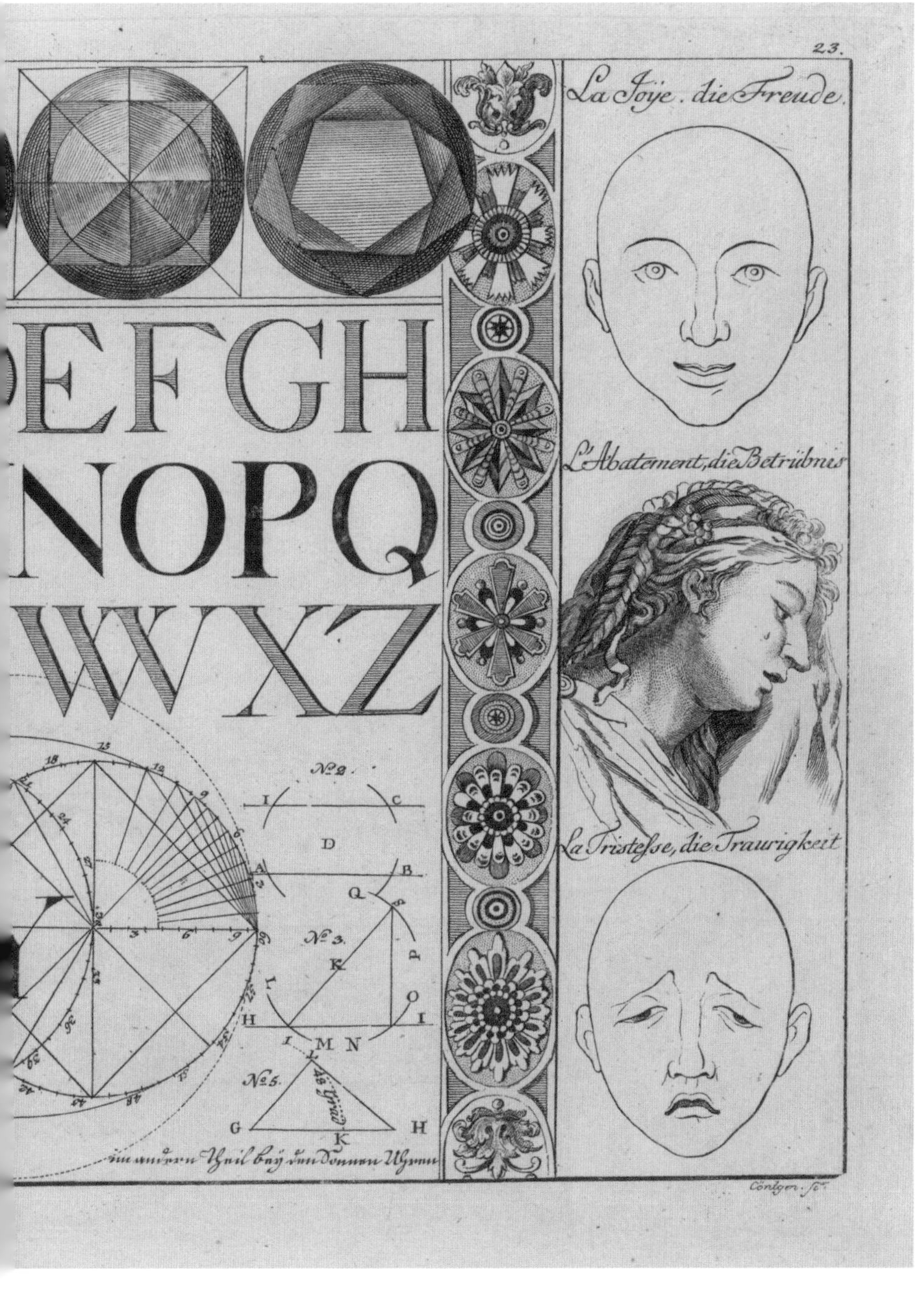
23.
La Joye. die Freude.
L'Abatement, die Betrübnis
La Tristesse, die Traurigkeit
EFGH
NOPQ
WXZ

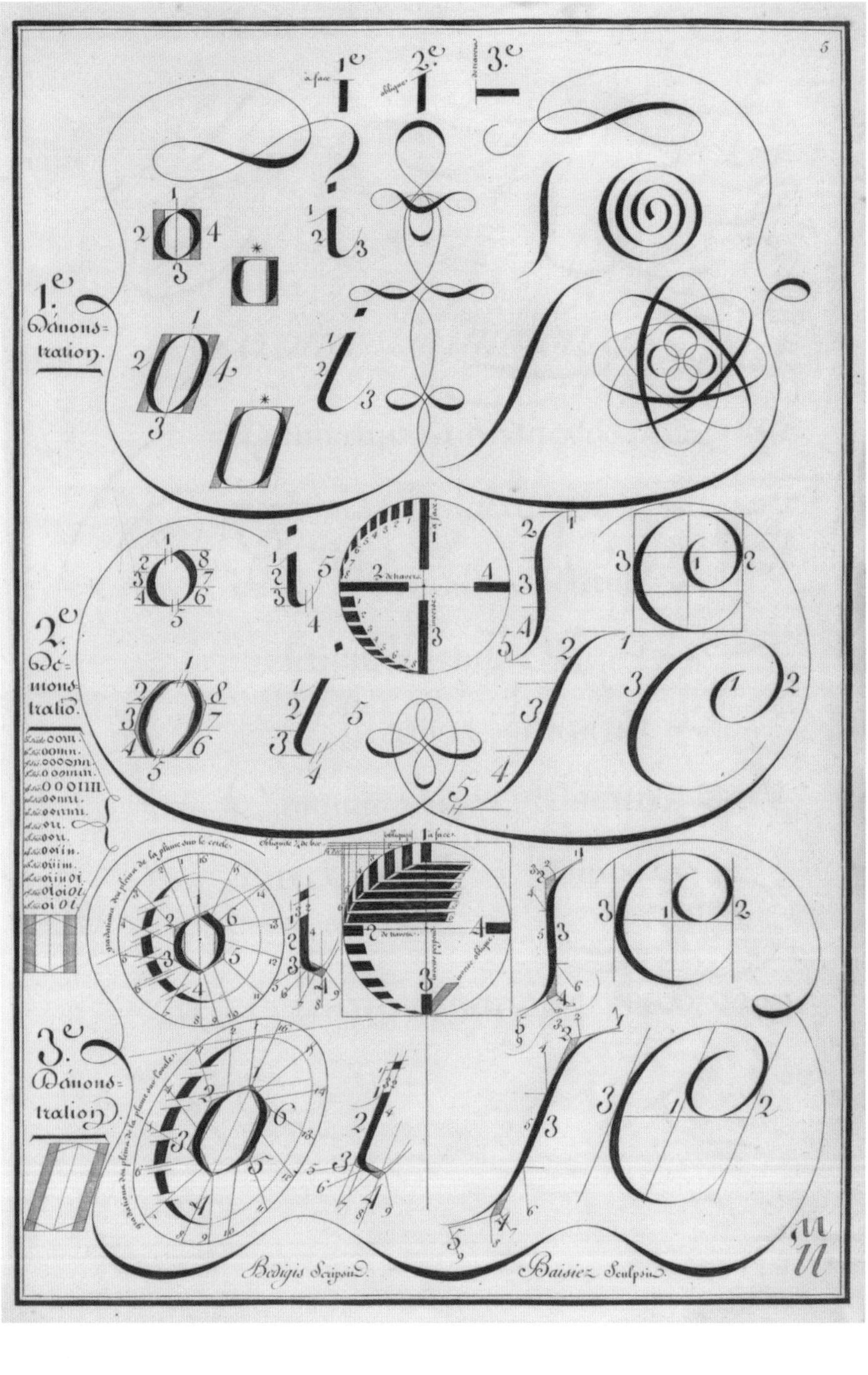
5
1.e Démonstration.
2.e Démonstration.
3.e Démonstration.
Bedigis Scripsit.
Baisiez Sculpsit.

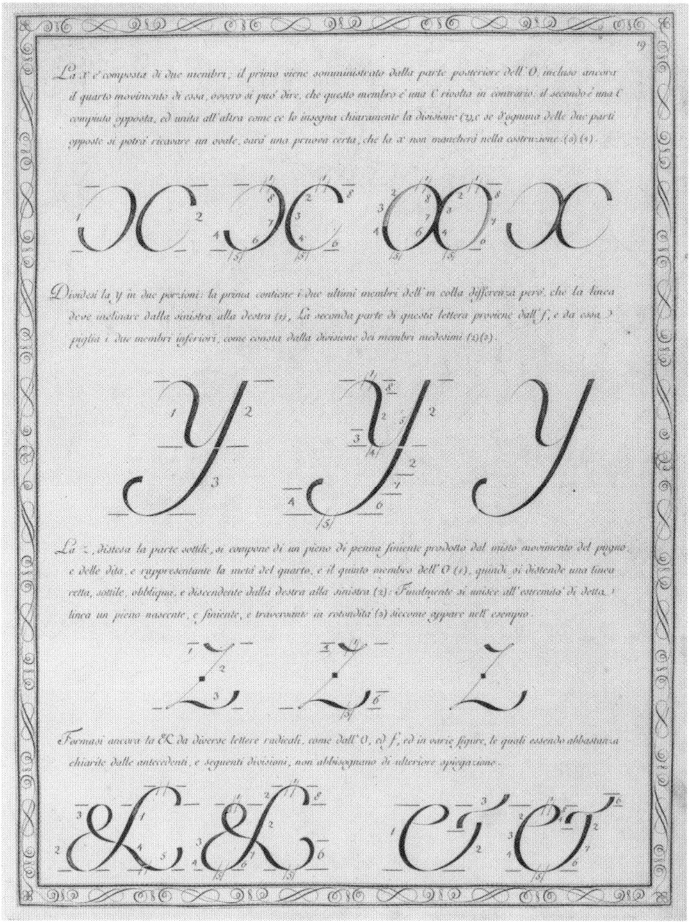

Fig. 1, previous spread: Plate from Johann Merken, *Liber artificiosvs alphabeti maioris* (Elberfield and Mülheim am Rhein, 1782–1785), a writing book.

TypW 720.82.567, plate 23, Houghton Library, Harvard University.

Fig. 2, opposite: Plate from François Nicolas Bédigis, *L'art d'écrire* (Paris: Butard, 1768).

TypW 815.0.198, plate 5, Houghton Library, Harvard University.

Fig. 3, above: Plate from engraved copy book illustrating the structure of lowercase cursive letters x through z and an ampersand (Roman on the right and italic on the left). F. Decaroli, *Decaroli, Ammaestramenti… d' imparare da per se la scrittura* (Turin: Decaroli, 1772).

TypW 725.72.319, plate 19, Houghton Library, Harvard University.

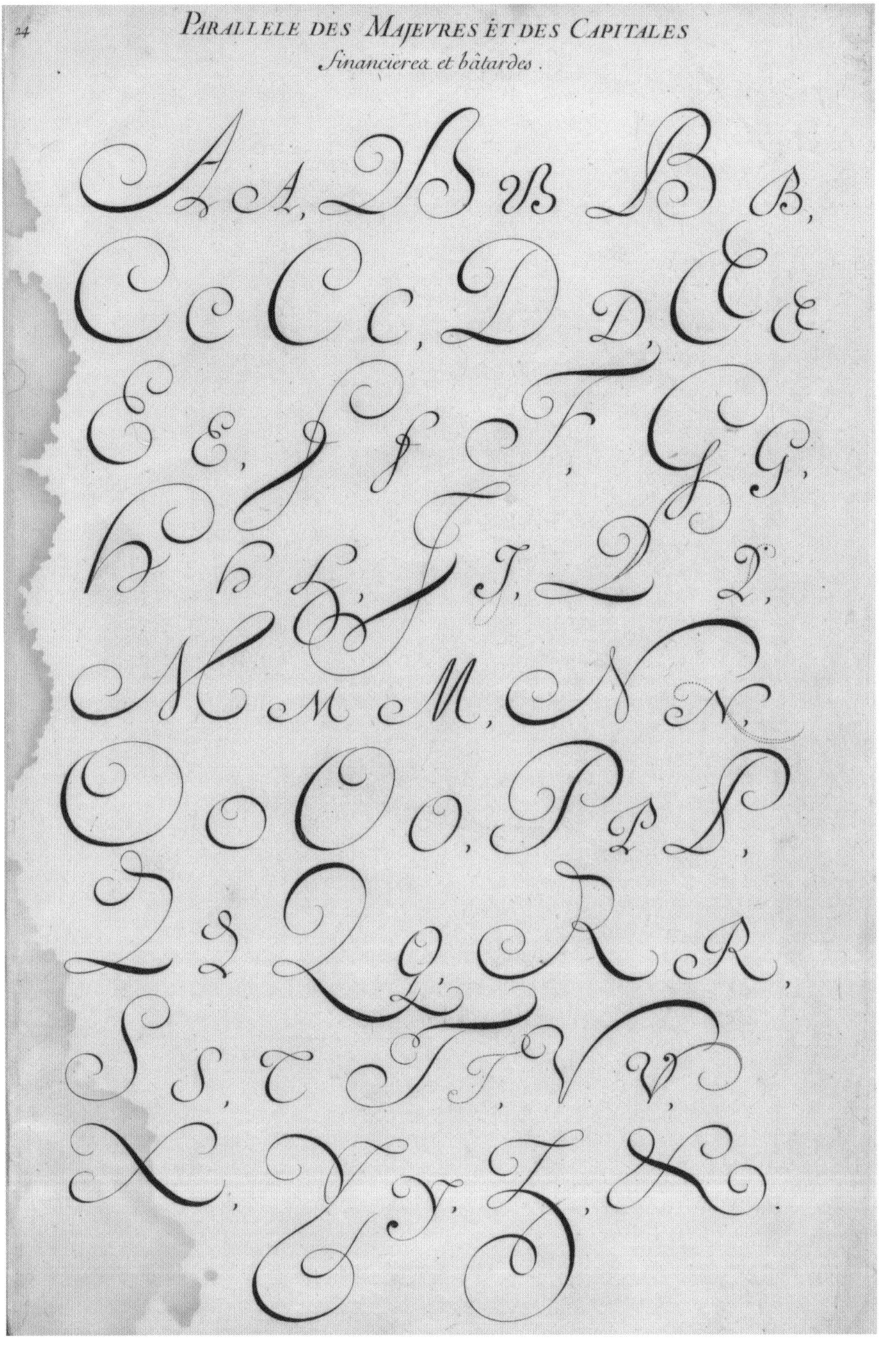
24
PARALLELE DES MAJEVRES ET DES CAPITALES
financieres et bâtardes.

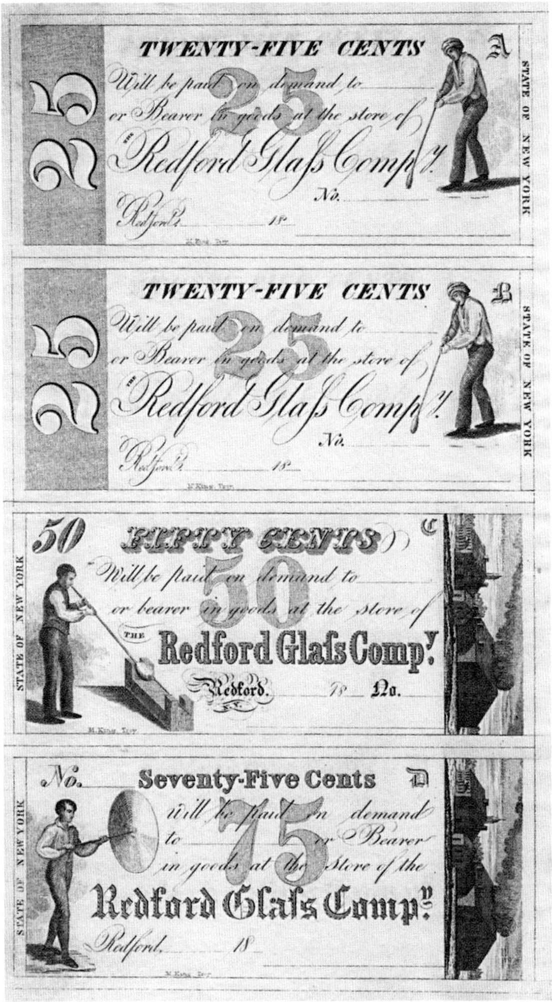
TWENTY-FIVE CENTS
A
Will be paid on demand to
or Bearer in goods at the store of
Redford Glafs Compy.
No.
Redford 18
STATE OF NEW YORK
TWENTY-FIVE CENTS
B
Will be paid on demand to
or Bearer in goods at the store of
Redford Glafs Compy.
No.
Redford 18
STATE OF NEW YORK
50
FIFTY CENTS
C
Will be paid on demand to
or bearer in goods at the store of
THE Redford Glafs Compy.
Redford. 18 No.
STATE OF NEW YORK
No.
Seventy-Five Cents
D
will be paid on demand
to or Bearer
in goods at the Store of the
Redford Glafs Compy.
Redford. 18
STATE OF NEW YORK

Fig. 4, opposite:
Engraved plate from Jean-Baptiste Allais, *L'Art d'écrire par Allais* (Paris: Allais, 1688).
TypW 615.80.134, plate 24, Houghton Library, Harvard University.

Fig. 5, above:
Engraved script redeemable at the Redford Glass Company store, Redford, New York (1830–1851).
Collection of Richard D. Sheaff.

a little more than fifty years, roughly from before the Civil War to the end of the nineteenth century, when photography became the more cost-effective method for illustration.

During this period, and through the turn of the twentieth century, while legions of engravers, printers, and print jobbers established successful careers, the small, burgeoning industry of social stationery began to evolve.[2] Also known as letter papers or society papers, social stationery included but was not limited to personal letters and notes, note cards, visiting cards, at home cards, calling cards, monograms and ciphers, invitations, condolence cards, thank-you notes, acknowledgments, and announcements. [**Figs. 6, 7**]

> I have now attained the true art of letter-writing, which we are always told, is to express on paper exactly what one would say to the same person by word of mouth; I have been talking to you almost as fast as I could the whole of this letter.[3]
> —Jane Austen

In the days before computers, e-mail, and smart phones, people communicated written thoughts, emotions, and ideas through a letter or its shorter form, a note. Since the Sumerians brought us writing more than five thousand years ago, whole industries have emerged for the creation of ingenious paper products—stationery—that could transmit these handwritten, hand-set, and, later, typed messages.

Traditionally, the highest form of stationery has always been engraved. With the rise of the middle class during the Industrial Revolution, personal stationery became an important means for people to improve their social status. Individuals, households, and businesses that wanted to gain access to successively loftier and more cultivated circles commissioned customized letterheads, calling cards, and other letter papers. A hardworking young man, for example, with aspirations of improving his station in life might marry a like-minded young woman, and together they would climb, rung by rung, to the

MISTICK KREWE OF COMUS
1877
TUESDAY EVE. FEB. 13TH
COMUS WELCOMES YOU TO HIS
FESTIVAL

Krewe of Proteus
French Opera House
Monday, February twenty fifth,
1895.

Fig. 6, left:
Mistick Krew of Comus, engraved invitation with gold metallic lithography (New Orleans, 1877).
The Historic New Orleans Collection, accession no. 1974.25.19.491

Fig. 7, right:
Mardi Gras invitation for the Krew of Proteus, engraved (New Orleans, 1895). Carnival invitations produced in New Orleans were generally much showier and garish chromolithography or offset lithography with elaborate die cuts produced locally, but a few examples of these more sedate styles exist, perhaps engraved in New York or elsewhere.
The Historic New Orleans Collection, accession no.1974.25.19.616

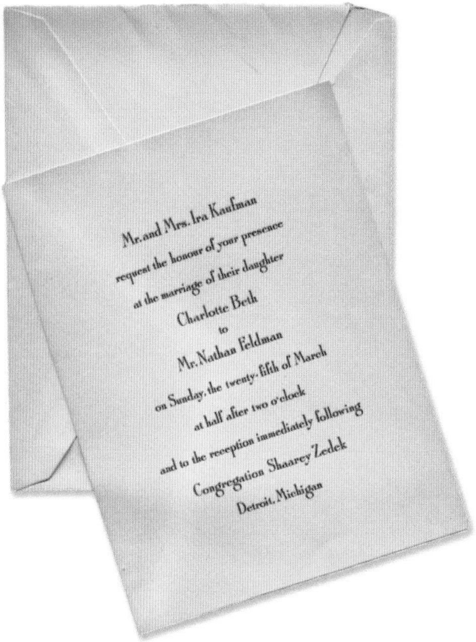
Mr. and Mrs. Ira Kaufman
request the honour of your presence
at the marriage of their daughter
Charlotte Beth
to
Mr. Nathan Feldman
on Sunday, the twenty-fifth of March
at half after two o'clock
and to the reception immediately following
Congregation Shaarey Zedek
Detroit, Michigan

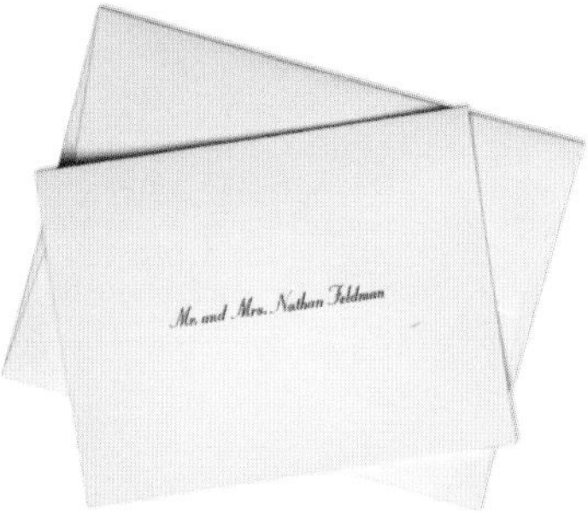
Mr. and Mrs. Nathan Feldman

Proper forms
APPROVED FORMS

Fig. 8, left:
Engraved invitation to the wedding of the author's parents (Detroit, 1951). The typeface is Masterplate Style Antique Text No. B-216 (see page 177).

Fig. 9, top right:
Engraved note cards for the author's newly wedded parents (Detroit, 1951). The typeface is Masterplate Style St. James No. 62 (see page 177).

Fig. 10, bottom right:
Trade manuals for the proper design and use of engraved social stationery: *Proper forms of engraving for social usage, Engraved Stationery Manufacturers Association* (1952) and *Approved forms for engraved stationery*, Z. & W. M. Crane, Inc. (Dalton, 1938).

> THE SUCCESSFUL TRANSMISSION OF A MESSAGE THROUGH A NOTE OR LETTER IS AT THE HEART OF SOCIAL, AND CIVIC, INTERACTION. LIKE A HUG OR MEANINGFUL HANDSHAKE, IT IS THE PHYSICAL EXPRESSION OF HOW WE FEEL TOWARD EACH OTHER.

upwardly mobile middle class and beyond. [**Figs. 8, 9**] One of the essential passports for this ascent was (and, in some circles, still is) appropriate social stationery as well as the knowledge of how to write a proper thank-you note, letter of congratulations, or condolence card. Social stationery and engraving played a vital role in the literature of socially conscious writers of the time, such as Arthur Schnitzler, Henry James, and Edith Wharton. Even Jack London's semiautobiographical figure, Martin Eden, in his book by the same name, frets over the correct use of calling cards while courting a young lady. This is particularly surprising because London is better known for outdoor-adventure swaggering than the minutiae of parlor manners, and indicates the importance of social customs during those days.

From the thirteenth to the fifteenth centuries, when few people knew how to read, let alone write, the term *stationer* referred to a stationary (a geographically fixed establishment), where one could have a letter written, commission a manuscript, or (if you could write) purchase writing implements, such as a pen or a pot of ink. Stationers were responsible for the way writing looked, acted, and felt. [**Fig. 10**]

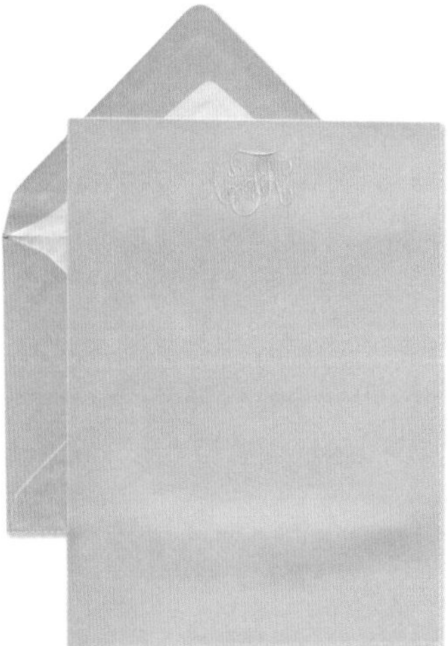

Fig. 11, opposite, top: Engraved bridal cipher for the author's mother on Crane & Co. paper (Detroit, 1951). The cipher is ribbon style, created by engraving multiple lines contouring in the same direction.
Estate of Charlotte Kaufman Feldman. The original plate was lost in the early 1980s.

Fig. 12, opposite, bottom left: Replica of original cipher engraved on Pineider note sheets.
Engraved for the author, New York, early 1980s.

Fig. 13, opposite, bottom right: Replica of original cipher engraved in the ribbon style. Note that the engraving is not as delicate as the original. Bold ink and paper color choices were used to compensate for the lack of refinement.
Engraved for the author, New York, early 1980s.

Fig. 14, above: Press proof of replicated plate for Charlotte Kaufman Feldman cipher. Note that the delicate interior lines are no longer present.
Engraved for the author, New York, early 1980s.

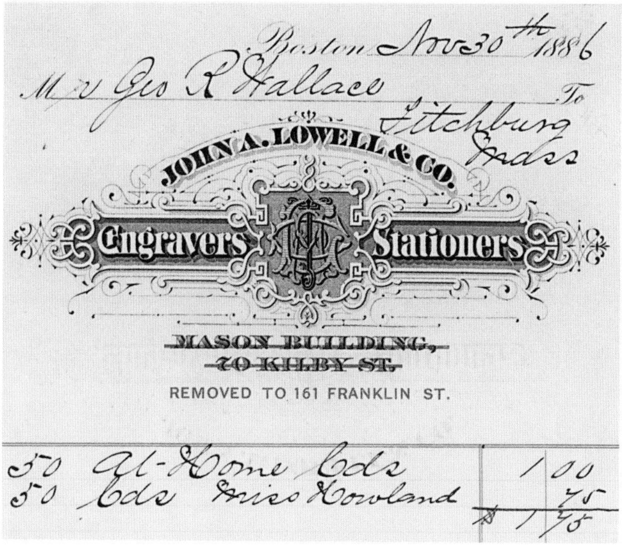
Boston Nov 30th 1886
Mr Geo R Wallace
To
Fitchburg
Mass
JOHN A. LOWELL & CO.
Engravers Stationers
~~MASON BUILDING,~~
~~70 KILBY ST.~~
REMOVED TO 161 FRANKLIN ST.

50 At-Home Cds	1	00
50 Cds Miss Howland		75
	$ 1	75

LONG MEADOW
SOUTH PARAMUS ROAD
RIDGEWOOD, NEW JERSEY
forty-seven poplar street
northport, long island, n.y.
428 Walton Road
South Orange, New Jersey
FORTY WEST FIFTY-SIXTH STREET
NEW YORK CITY
WILLIAM C. PARKER
824 Madison Avenue
EDWARD G. WARREN
FOUR HUNDRED AND EIGHT PARK AVENUE
GEORGE W. BARROWS
Cedar Grove
Stamford, Connecticut
THE SHADOWS
Miami, Florida
Northeast Harbor
Maine
haversham house
aiken, south carolina
EIGHTY WEST FIFTY-NINTH STREET
NEW YORK CITY
108-12 Puritan Avenue
Forest Hills Gardens
Long Island
JAMES GRANTLAND SMYTH
GARDEN CITY, NEW YORK
five sixty park avenue
173 SOMERSET STREET
BANGOR, MAINE
206 kensington road
garden city, long island
71 CENTRAL PARK WEST

Until recently, stationers were commonplace in the United States and Western Europe. Traditionally, the stationer helped his customers announce the important passages in life, such as births, marriages, mourning services, and the opening and closing of businesses. [**Figs. 11–14**] The stationer was, in a way, the gatekeeper of local social norms who would (delicately) let you know, "Oh, no, my dear, one would never use that color for one's coming-out announcement." Some stationers printed on their own small presses kept in the back of the store, but most maintained accounts with regional and national engraving and stationery firms for custom work beyond their means. [**Figs. 15, 16**]

Modern stationery is paper (or stock) cut to specific dimensions and sold in a standardized system of sizes. Standardization is important for manufacturing, marketing, and merchandising in any volume. The more a printer can manufacture of one size and kind, the cheaper the per-unit production cost. Without standard sizes and measures of volume, handsome packaging at affordable pricing—now widely available in chain stores such as Target, Crane & Co., Walmart, and Hallmark—would not be possible. Devoted stationers offering engraving can still be found today; however, as time goes on and rent and overhead costs increase, fewer and fewer survive.

Fig. 15, opposite, top: Engraved billhead of the engraving and stationery company John A. Lowell & Co, 1886.
Collection of Richard D. Sheaff.

Fig. 16, opposite, bottom: Samples of engraved lettering styles. New York, probably 1950s or 1960s.

Chapter Two

A BRIEF HISTORY OF STATIONERY PAPER AND THE MAIL

Paper was invented in the first part of the second century in China, from where it spread to Korea and Japan. The art of papermaking, and the craftsmen who hand-made each sheet, were held in high esteem. Paper was not offered or shared easily.[1] It was not until 751 BCE that the method made its way to the Middle East, where, in a battle, Arabs captured Chinese warriors proficient in papermaking and forced them to explain their craft in exchange for freedom. Advances in papermaking, writing (calligraphy at that time), and bookmaking were made in the Arab world while Europeans were still using dried animal skin (parchment) to write on. It was not until the 1200s, when European Christians made war on Islamist Spain, that they won knowledge of papermaking.

Oriental paper was primarily made from vegetable fiber abundant in the East but unavailable in substantial quality and quantity in Europe. The first Western paper was made from cloth rags. In the papermaking process, the fiber (derived from vegetable matter, cloth rags, or wood) must be reduced to pulp before it can be molded into sheets and dried. Early European pulp may have contained bits of wood and straw—cheaper and more readily available than rags—which were collected by tradesmen from the general population and then sold to papermakers. The process of pulping wood for paper took centuries to develop, because it was much too difficult and impractical for generalized use.

The development of writing and writing tools also differed between the East and the West. Calligraphy in the East was accomplished with a brush, while Europeans learned to write with a pen. This distinction dictated the way paper evolved, because the softer writing surface compatible with a brush is very different from the harder sheet necessary for writing with a pen.[2]

The paper Gutenberg used was originally produced for the purposes of writing, because printing did not yet exist. As innovations in writing pens and printing progressed, so did the production of paper for personal and commercial use. Both paper and writing technologies evolved in the ensuing centuries depending on available resources, money, and the occasional interruption (and innovations) resulting from war. With the Industrial Revolution and the invention of wood-pulping processes in the mid-nineteenth century, the manufacturing of paper became significantly cheaper and developed into a commodity for the masses. It was during that time that stationery became an important part of social life. An industry for personal stationery and letter papers grew, helped by the popularization of the department store and the point-of-purchase display in the mid-1800s.

Prior to that time the local general store provided much of what customers couldn't grow or produce themselves: flour, salt, coffee, fabric, nails, tools, shoes, and other supplies. Nothing was prepackaged, and every product, sold by the pound, inch, or yard, had to be weighed or measured. Typically, the customer handed a list of items needed to the shopkeeper, who stood behind a sales counter. The counter separated the client from most of the goods.

Therefore, when the first department stores were developed, with goods put out on the selling floor in elaborate displays to encourage shoppers to touch, feel, and interact with the merchandise, a degree of intimacy was established. Customers felt free to browse and shop independently. The concept of shopping transformed from purchasing staples, such as food and soap, to buying nonessential merchandise for the sake of pleasure, including stationery and letter papers.[3] Rooms well stocked with paper products and pens were provided, so women could relax and write letters.[4]

In 1843 the first commercial Christmas card was produced. With the invention of Flexography (a printing process that uses flexible relief plates to accommodate thick boards or stiff papers) in 1890 and offset lithography for paper in 1904 or 1905, possibilities for decorative wrapping papers and gift boxes facilitated a growing interest in store-bought stationery. Selecting stationery and perfecting the skills of letter writing became a right of social passage, and the product itself evolved into a commodity. [**Fig. 1**]

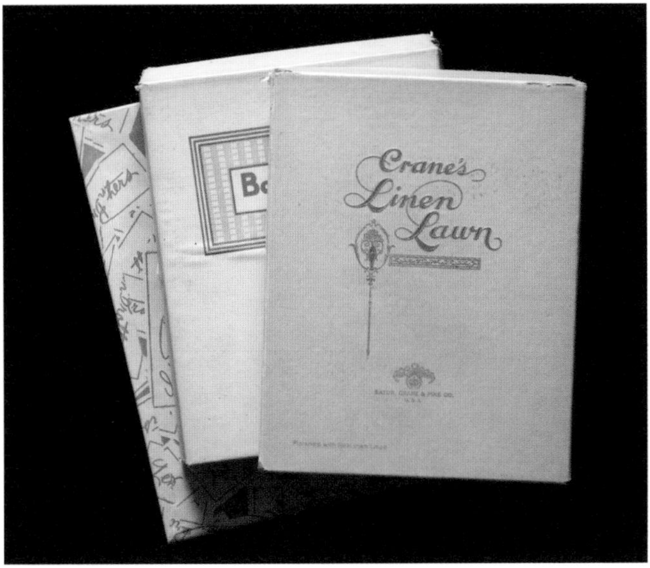
Crane's
Linen
Lawn

Fig. 1:
Vintage boxed sets of stationery.

The way of delivering these personal letters and other correspondence has also changed significantly over the centuries. Though once prohibitively expensive for the general population, a version of the postal service has been with us since biblical times. For centuries, a folded letter could be sent directly through the mail system. Since the number of sheets determined the rate, wrapping a letter with a protective covering of any kind was considered wasteful.[5] Enclosing a letter in an envelope did not become a practical notion in Great Britain or the United States until the 1800s. [**Fig. 2**]

In 1837 a British postal reformer by the name of Rowland Hill conceived of a uniform preprinted envelope and prepaid postage in the form of adhesive stamps, thereby shifting payment to the sender rather than the receiver, as had been the norm.[6] He believed that mailing a letter should be affordable for everyone and that a uniform system would prevent corruption.The first stamps, known as the Penny Black and

Brainerd & Burridge,
ENGRAVERS,
Designers & Lithographers;
HERALD BLOCK, CLEVELAND, O.
CLEVELAND O.
MAY
7
3 PAID

W. MULREADY, R.A.
POSTAGE ONE PENNY.
JOHN THOMPSON

Fig. 2, top: Engraved cover, early 1850s.
Collection of Richard D. Sheaff.

Fig. 3, bottom: Mulready envelope.
Collection of John Tingey.

the Two Penny Blue, which feature an engraved profile of the young Queen Victoria by Henry Corbould printed in black ink and blue ink, respectively, were issued in 1840. The rate was one cent for each half ounce. The prepaid envelope became known as a Mulready, after the artist whose drawing adorned the front.[7] [**Fig. 3**] William Mulready's design pictured Britannia as a goddesslike individual, central in a panorama of characters depicting communication powers that, by century's end, would nearly span the world. This allegorical illustration was derided for its overstated patriotism; spoofs of the artwork were widely circulated and are now quite collectible. The Mulready envelope was removed from circulation in 1841, but the use of stamps and the envelope as a postal medium thrived. Today's adhesive-backed postage stamps and preprinted postal envelopes are the descendants of Hill's efforts.

By the mid-nineteenth century, sending a half-ounce letter across America cost as little as three cents.[8] Standardization and inexpensive service fostered increased use of the postal system, popularizing the need for envelopes and encouraging innovation by the companies that manufactured them. In the early 1850s, the development of the envelope-folding machine (one version of which was invented by Rowland Hill's older brother, Edwin) automated the process of stacking individual sheets, trimming with the use of a template, assembling, and gluing. The oldest continuously operating envelope company in the United States, Berlin & Jones, credits its longevity to the firm's openness to new technology, dating from the purchase of an automated envelope machine at the Paris Exposition in 1856.[9]

However, technological innovations in recent decades have contributed to the decline of letter writing. The speedy transmissions of facsimile (fax) and electronic communications (e-mail and text messaging) have reduced the need for postal services.[10] Nevertheless, the art of letter writing is experiencing a renaissance, as letters sent through the mail are cherished as something special in our digital age.

Chapter Three

COMPONENTS AND ETIQUETTE OF SOCIAL STATIONERY

Once you embark on assembling your own set of engraved social stationery, you may be overwhelmed at first by the myriad paper products available. There are sheets for writing formal correspondence, casual thoughts, and sweet missives; there are visiting, note, and business cards; and there are big envelopes and tiny ones. Stationery can be purchased as individual pieces or in sets. Nothing beats letter paper with your own name engraved upon it, but what form of social stationery should you choose?

CALLING CARDS AND VISITING CARDS

> To the unrefined or underbred, the visiting card is but a trifling and insignificant bit of paper; but to the cultured disciple of social law, it conveys subtle and unmistakable intelligence.[1]
>
> —John H. Young, *A Guide to the Manners, Etiquette, and Deportment of the Most Refined Society*, 1879

Calling cards, or visiting cards, were traditionally small pieces of card stock bearing just an elegantly engraved name on the front, with no contact information. In the eighteenth, nineteenth, and early twentieth centuries, the miniscule missives, left with the servant at the front door, were the basis of social form and etiquette. Impeccable engraving on plain but excellent-quality paper in understated black ink was the requirement in polite society in America.

In those times, if you were born into (or aspired to become part of) the middle or upper class, it was your responsibility to make social calls to those receiving at home. This was an everyday affair, and there were certain hours when calls were appropriate and expected. In an age before the invention and widespread use of the telephone, one would "call on" others to make friends and socialize.[2] There were conventions to such social calls: it was considered improper for a young lady to call

QUESTION

What is the difference between a calling card and a visiting card?

ANSWER

NONE. VISITING CARDS AND CALLING CARDS SERVE THE SAME PURPOSE AND LOOK THE SAME.

alone, much easier for a married woman, and perfectly acceptable for all men. In general, however, it was more typical for women to do the calling, as visitation by a lone male could be construed as inappropriate.

But if a young man of the middle or upper class moved to a new town, carrying names and perhaps letters of introduction to luminaries of local businesses, he would first call upon the reigning matriarch of the community to introduce himself. If she approved of the young man, the matriarch, in turn, would make proper introductions to other important individuals. The man would take great care dressing for his visit, sure to appear conservative enough for the most restrained and sharp enough to be noticed. A designated butler would answer his ringing of the bell at the front door, accept his calling card, and transfer it within the inner workings of the house. Only intimates and those already accepted into the prominent circles of the local society were received on a first visit, which is why these little paper gems were also called visiting cards. This ritual was a prelude to, or a substitution for, in-person exchanges.[3]

Calling cards could be personalized with a note or an address by hand. One custom was to strike out the engraved name and sign the name by which you wanted to be referred. Specific coded meaning could be conveyed through the folding of corners: an unfolded card meant that it was delivered by a servant; a fold of the upper right-hand corner meant that someone had visited in person; a fold of the upper left-hand corner conveyed congratulations or felicitation; and a fold of the lower left-hand corner expressed condolence or was done to say good-bye. "P.P.C." (*pour prendre congé*, "for leave-taking"), written on the lower right-hand corner, indicated that someone was taking leave (perhaps leaving town for the summer season). As the convention was to return a call with a call (or accept the initial caller on his or her next visit), an unreturned card or, worse, a card that was returned in an envelope meant that the caller's social advances were not accepted—please do not call again.[4]

At the turn of the twentieth century, calling cards were cherished for their emotional significance and innuendo and collected in scrapbooks.[5] [**Fig. 1**] Today, calling cards are enjoying a revival. We don't go calling anymore, and we no longer fold the corners up or down, but these little wonders can still convey notes and messages in a personal way. [**Fig. 2**] A contemporary calling card functions equally well in casual, formal, or intimate social interactions. They "differ from conventional business cards in that they provide as little information as possible.... These cards don't shout; they flirt—with potential employers, contacts and even love interests."[6] [**Figs. 3, 4**] When meeting someone

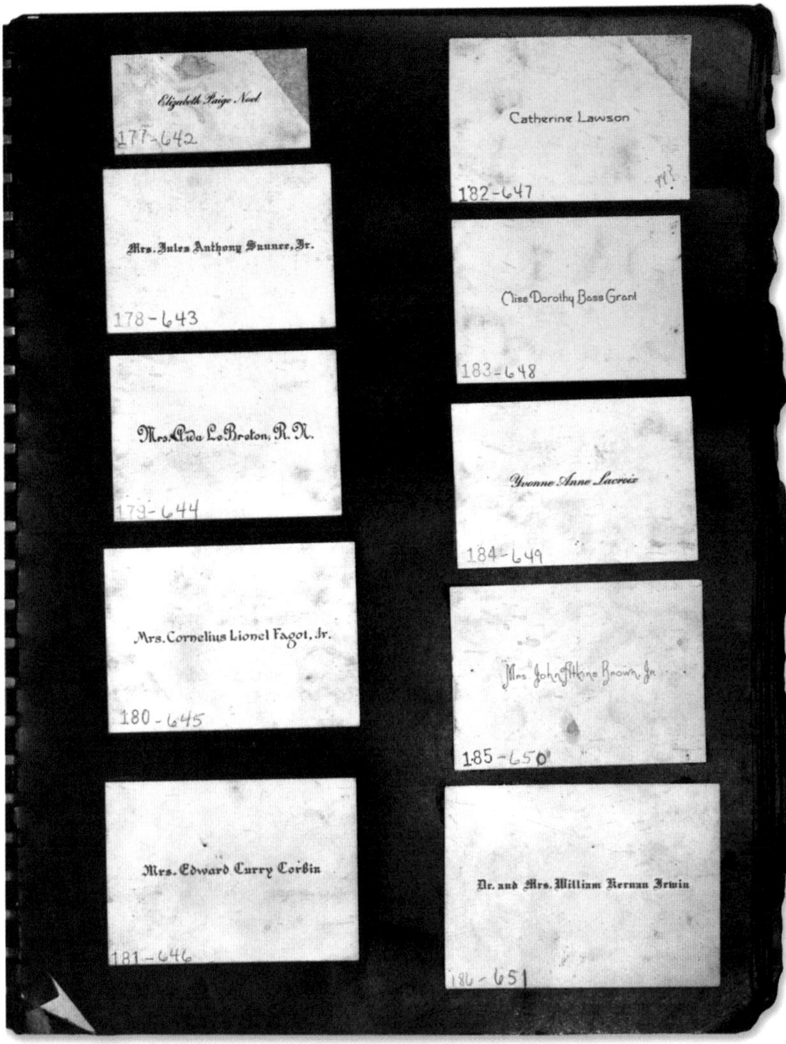
Elizabeth Paige Noel
177-642
Catherine Lawson
182-647
Mrs. Jules Anthony Sanner, Jr.
178-643
Miss Dorothy Bass Grant
183-648
Mrs. Ada Le Breton, R.N.
179-644
Yvonne Anne Lacroix
184-649
Mrs. Cornelius Lionel Fagot, Jr.
180-645
Mrs. John Atkins Brown, Jr.
185-650
Mrs. Edward Curry Corbin
181-646
Dr. and Mrs. William Kernan Irwin
186-651

Fig. 1:
Examples of engraved calling cards, ca. 1930s–1970s, from a sample book of engraved stationery items.
Lehman Brothers Inc., New Haven, Connecticut.

CONVENTIONS

CARD RETURNED UNFOLDED:

PLEASE DO NOT CALL AGAIN

....

UPPER RIGHT-HAND CORNER FOLDED:

SOMEONE HAS VISITED IN PERSON

....

UPPER LEFT-HAND CORNER FOLDED:

CONGRATULATIONS

OR

FELICITATION

....

LOWER LEFT-HAND CORNER FOLDED:

CONDOLENCE

OR

TO SAY GOOD-BYE

....

"P.P.C." WRITTEN ON LOWER RIGHT-HAND CORNER:

SOMEONE IS TAKING LEAVE

....

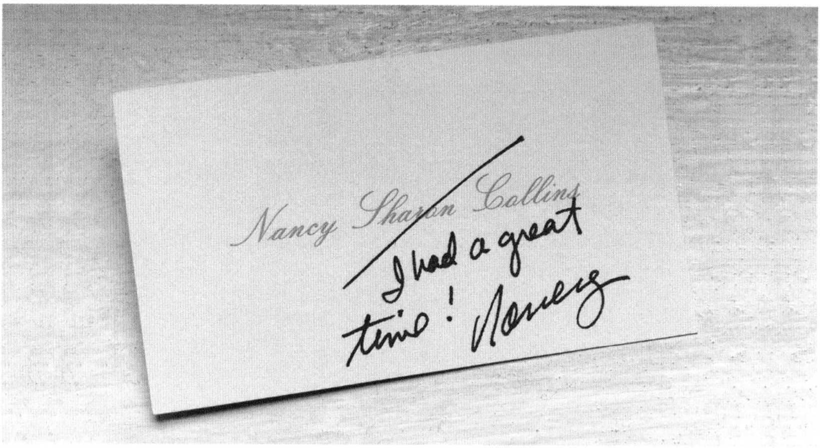
Nancy Sharon Collins
I had a great time! Nancy

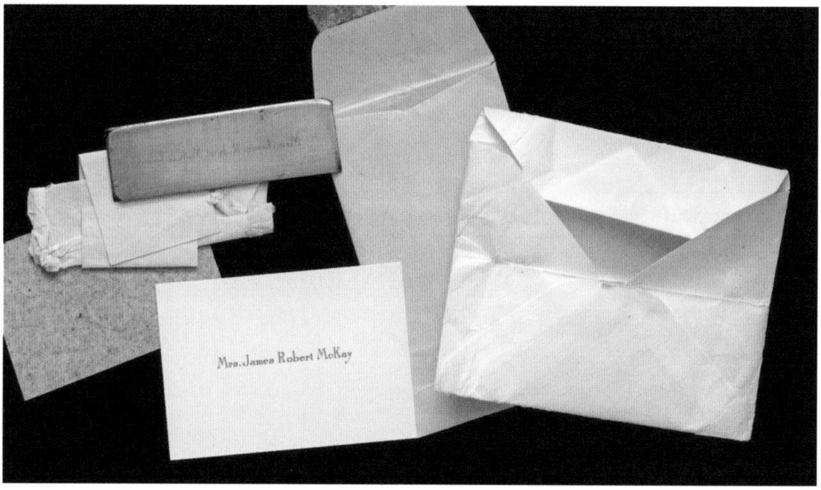
Mrs. James Robert McKay

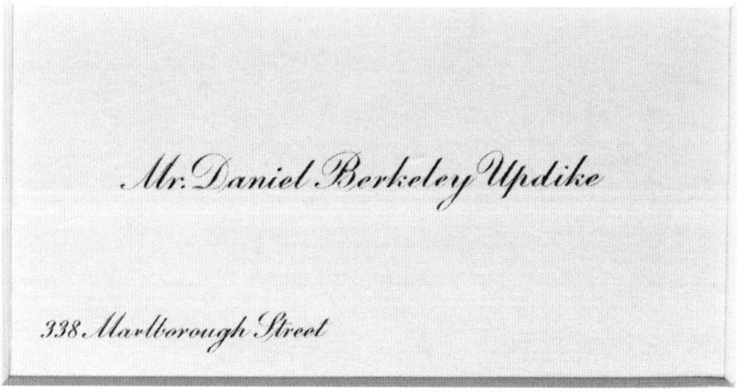
Mr. Daniel Berkeley Updike
338 Marlborough Street

Miss Dorothy Davis Ball
Florence Cohn
Deborah Joy Shelton

Fig. 2, opposite, top: Photoengraved calling card with personal message to a friend handwritten with fountain pen by the author.

Fig. 3, opposite, middle: Engraved steel plate, tissue wrapper, manila envelope, and calling card for Mrs. J. R. McKay, ca. 1940s–1950s. The calling card was a requisite item of social etiquette for a Navy officer's wife. The card is engraved in Masterplate Style Artisan Roman No. 49.

Fig. 4, opposite, bottom: Engraved calling card of printer and scholar of type and printing history Daniel Berkeley Updike (1860–1941) (London?: engraver and printer unknown, ca. 1920s–1930s). It is interesting that this card, rather than being produced by Updike's own Merrymount Press, or any other letterpress, was engraved.
Collection of Martin Hutner. Photo by Mark Schreyer, 2011.

Fig. 5, above: Three examples of calling cards. The one on the right is letterpress-printed and illustrates the card's use as a communication tool. It was the property of the author's maternal grandmother and is signed in her grandfather's hand. The other two are engraved; the one on the left also has a blind-debossed panel.

STEVEN L. FEINBERG'S *CRANE'S BLUE BOOK OF STATIONERY* LISTS THE FOLLOWING SIZES AS APPROPRIATE FOR VARIOUS KINDS OF CALLING CARDS:[7]

FOR A

Single Woman

2 7/8 X 2 INCHES

FOR A

Married Woman

3 1/8 X 2 1/4 INCHES

FOR A

Child

$2^1/_4$ X $1^3/_8$ INCHES

FOR A

Man

$3^3/_8$ X $1^1/_2$ INCHES

OR

$3^1/_2$ X 2 INCHES

FOR A

Married Couple

$3^3/_8$ X $2^1/_2$ INCHES

for the first time, you can personalize a calling card with the quick flick of a fountain pen by adding your home phone number if you like the person; giving your work number if you are not sure; jotting down your cell phone number if you really like the person; or making up a number if you never want to hear from them but don't want to appear impolite. You may wish to include your e-mail and home address, as well as links to various social media accounts. [**Fig. 5**]

AT HOME CARDS

Though rarely used today, at home cards were once used to announce a move into a new residence, a marriage, or notice of cohabitation. The card lists the address of the dwelling and implies that the lady of the house will be receiving those wishing to make social calls. [**Fig. 6**]

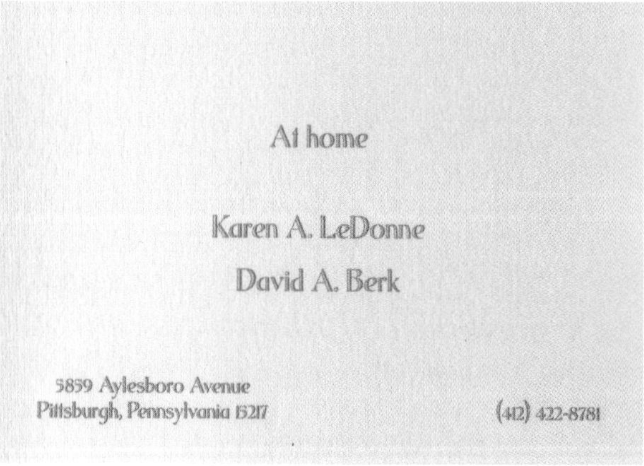
At home
Karen A. LeDonne
David A. Berk
5859 Aylesboro Avenue
Pittsburgh, Pennsylvania 15217
(412) 422-8781

Fig. 6:
Engraved at home card.
Client commission,
New York, ca. 2003.

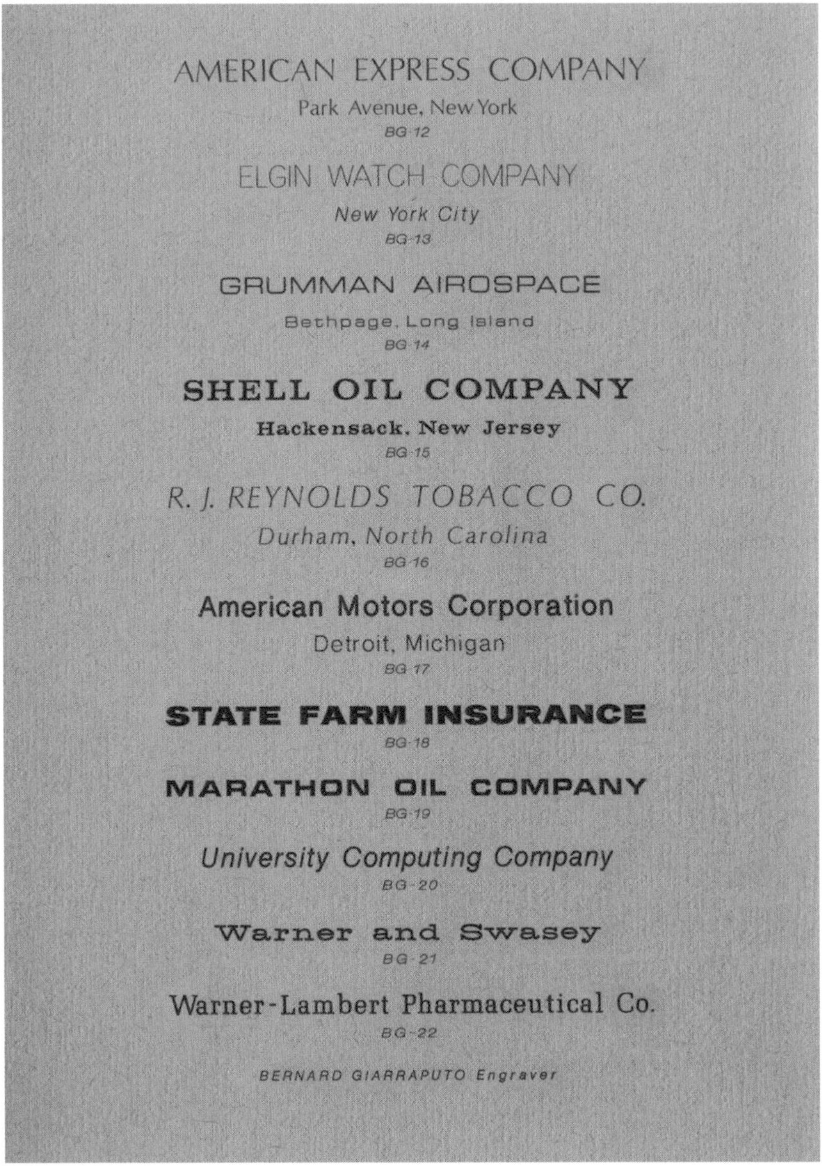
AMERICAN EXPRESS COMPANY
Park Avenue, New York
BG-12
ELGIN WATCH COMPANY
New York City
BG-13
GRUMMAN AIROSPACE
Bethpage, Long Island
BG-14
SHELL OIL COMPANY
Hackensack, New Jersey
BG-15
R. J. REYNOLDS TOBACCO CO.
Durham, North Carolina
BG-16
American Motors Corporation
Detroit, Michigan
BG-17
STATE FARM INSURANCE
BG-18
MARATHON OIL COMPANY
BG-19
University Computing Company
BG-20
Warner and Swasey
BG-21
Warner-Lambert Pharmaceutical Co.
BG-22
BERNARD GIARRAPUTO Engraver

Fig. 7:
Sample card of lettering styles for engraved stationery, ca. 1950s–1970s, New York.

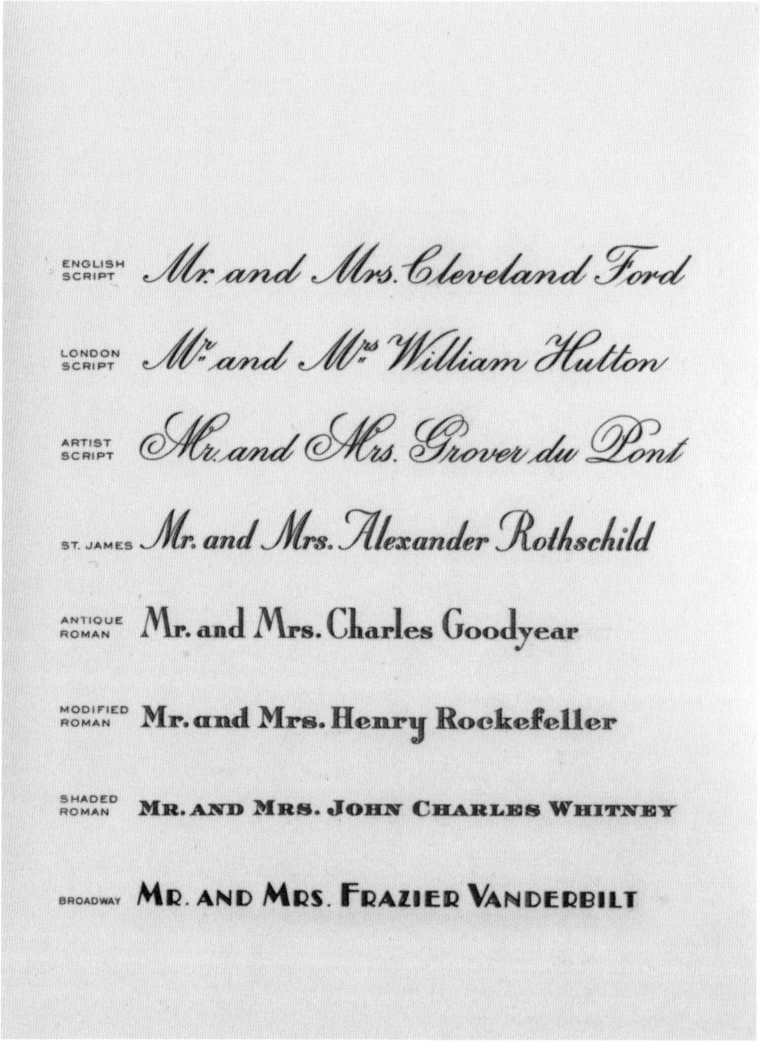
ENGLISH SCRIPT
Mr. and Mrs. Cleveland Ford
LONDON SCRIPT
Mr and Mrs William Hutton
ARTIST SCRIPT
Mr. and Mrs. Grover du Pont
ST. JAMES
Mr. and Mrs. Alexander Rothschild
ANTIQUE ROMAN
Mr. and Mrs. Charles Goodyear
MODIFIED ROMAN
Mr. and Mrs. Henry Rockefeller
SHADED ROMAN
MR. AND MRS. JOHN CHARLES WHITNEY
BROADWAY
MR. AND MRS. FRAZIER VANDERBILT

Fig. 8:
Sample card of lettering styles for engraved stationery, ca. 1950s–1970s, New York.

STATIONERY AND LETTER PAPERS

> "Writing a note or letter, the word of regret, the prompt or delayed answering of an invitation, the manner of salutation, the neglect of a required attention, all betray to the well-bred the degree or the absence of good breeding."
> —John H. Young, *A Guide to the Manners, Etiquette, and Deportment of the Most Refined Society*, 1879

A complete contemporary stationery set should contain note cards, letter sheets, monarch sheets, and note sheets. Note cards range in size from informal cards, approximately 5 × 3½ inches (fitting into the smallest envelope size that can be mailed in the United States), to supersized cards, measuring 5½ × 8½ (which fit inside an A9 envelope). [**Figs. 7–9**] A French folding card is similar to the formal letter sheet (discussed below); it is made with text-weight paper (rather than card stock) and folds once horizontally and once vertically, providing plenty of surface space for writing. Preprinted greeting cards were once made using this method. Note cards generally use uncoated stock, because it receives writing ink better than a glossy or coated paper. Fold-over notes are made of light card stock (approximately 60 to 80# cover) and usually come prescored to fold neatly.[8] Flat cards are usually 100# cover stock or heavier. Note sheets are folded once in half and are usually 24# to 32# writing paper.

Today, the most commonly used letter sizes in North America are 8½ × 11 inches (for commercial business letters) and slightly smaller monarch sheets (7¼ × 10½ inches) for home and domestic business. Both are folded in thirds and creased with a thumbnail or a bone folding knife.

Besides these standard sizes there are others to accommodate the cascading needs of personal correspondence. [**Fig. 10**] Generally speaking, informal communications can be handwritten on most anything,

Mr. and Mrs. William Preston Humphreys, III
request the honour of your presence
at the marriage of their daughter
Laura Natalie
to
John Peter Hudson, Jr.
son of
will attend
will not attend
The favor of a reply is requested before the fifteenth of March

Fig. 9:
While investing in a complete set of engraved stationery may be a stretch for many, ordering a monogram or cipher to be used by both bride and groom after marriage is a charming idea for newlyweds. This wedding suite includes an A7 note card engraved with the couple's marital cipher.

QUESTION

What are the necessary pieces in a contemporary stationery wardrobe?

ANSWER

NOTE CARDS,
LETTER SHEETS,
MONARCH SHEETS,
AND
NOTE SHEETS.

MONARCH SHEETS ARE PERFECT FOR WRITING A POLITE INQUIRY TO THE NEIGHBOR ABOUT WHY THE NEW DOG, OR NANNY, ACTS SO STRANGELY.

Fig. 10, above:
Examples of contemporary stationery envelopes. A pointed flap designates social use, except in a #10 business envelope, which may have either a square or pointed flap. The smallest envelope that the United States Postal Service will send is 5 x 3½ inches.

Fig. 11, opposite:
Photoengraved monarch-size hotel letterhead and envelope.

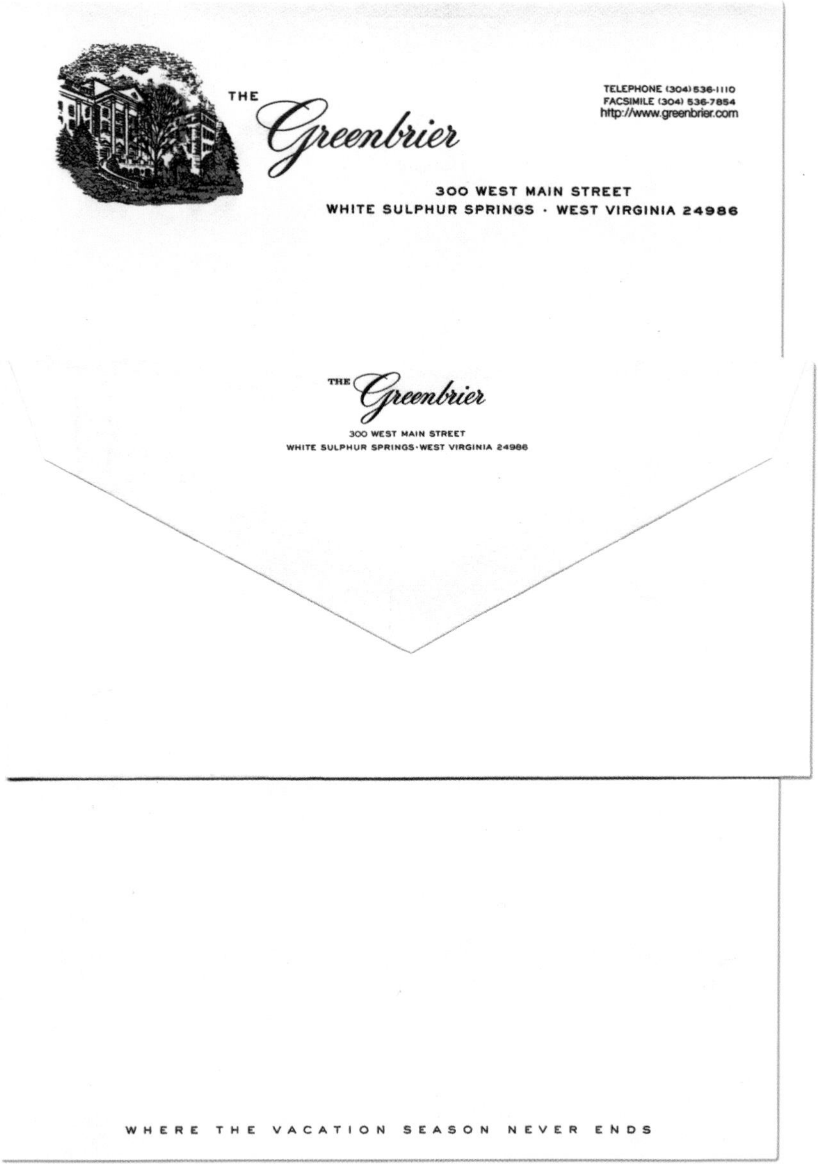
THE *Greenbrier*

TELEPHONE (304) 536-1110
FACSIMILE (304) 536-7854
http://www.greenbrier.com

300 WEST MAIN STREET
WHITE SULPHUR SPRINGS · WEST VIRGINIA 24986

THE *Greenbrier*

300 WEST MAIN STREET
WHITE SULPHUR SPRINGS·WEST VIRGINIA 24986

WHERE THE VACATION SEASON NEVER ENDS

Fig. 12:
Letter sheet engraved with a cipher. The envelope is blind embossed with "Cartier. New York, Paris, London." A barely discernible watermark on the lower left corner by the fold indicates that it was produced by Crane & Co. (for Cartier). Note that there is no border on the left side, which indicates that this is a folded letter sheet. The set was probably purchased at Cartier in New York, 1970s or later.

Fig. 13:
Engraved and embossed letterhead for the first female banker in the state of Louisiana. At the time of writing this book, Mary Serena Gibbens Borne, or Miss Weenie, as she is called by family members, friends, and intimates, is still an inveterate note writer at ninety-six years old. According to her granddaughter, Emily Delorge (an engraver, graphic designer, and herself a note writer), Miss Weenie's notes are legendary among those who know her. If typewritten, the note will probably be an admonishment for breeching some bit of moral etiquette known only in the unwritten book of Miss Weenie. If handwritten, there is a chance the recipient did something favorable.

Commissioned by Mrs. I. J. Borne, Thibodaux, Louisiana, date unknown.

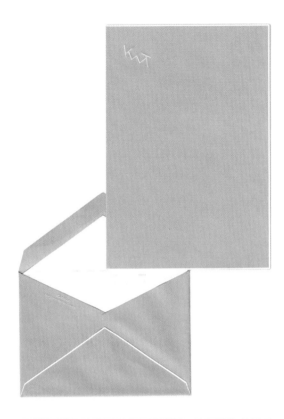

Lafourche National Bank of Thibodaux
THIBODAUX, LOUISIANA 70301

even if your handwriting is less than perfect. (Hotel stationery has long been a favorite for many.) [**Fig. 11**]

We once poured our hearts out into long, multipage, two-sided, handwritten letters. Now we e-mail or blog or follow each other on Facebook. I still maintain that there is nothing more welcome, personal, intimate, and discreet than receiving a handwritten letter or note in the mail. [**Figs. 12, 13**]

When corresponding socially, one should follow some simple rules for using the different pieces of available stationery:

Letter sheet: Letter sheets, which are rarely used anymore, are large pages, folded horizontally, then vertically, and slipped into an envelope one-quarter of the sheet size. [**Figs. 14, 16**] Formal wedding invitations still follow this format, and the front, or first, page faces the recipient as it is removed from the envelope, which should be opened from the back. [**Fig. 15**] The process of utilizing the quarters, or "pages," of the folded sheet is as follows:

First page of text (front cover)
Second page of text (inside back cover)
Third page of text (inside front cover)
Fourth page of text (back cover)

To replicate the effect without the expense of buying formal letter sheets, a quarter-folded business sheet (8½ × 11 inches) will fit into a commercially available 5½ bar envelope.

Monarch sheet: As the story goes, monarch letter papers are derived from a size once reserved for use by royalty. Currently, it is the most popular letter sheet used for social purposes. Only its front is written upon, never the back, requiring the use of second sheets for longer correspondence. These are the same size as the first sheet but usually come

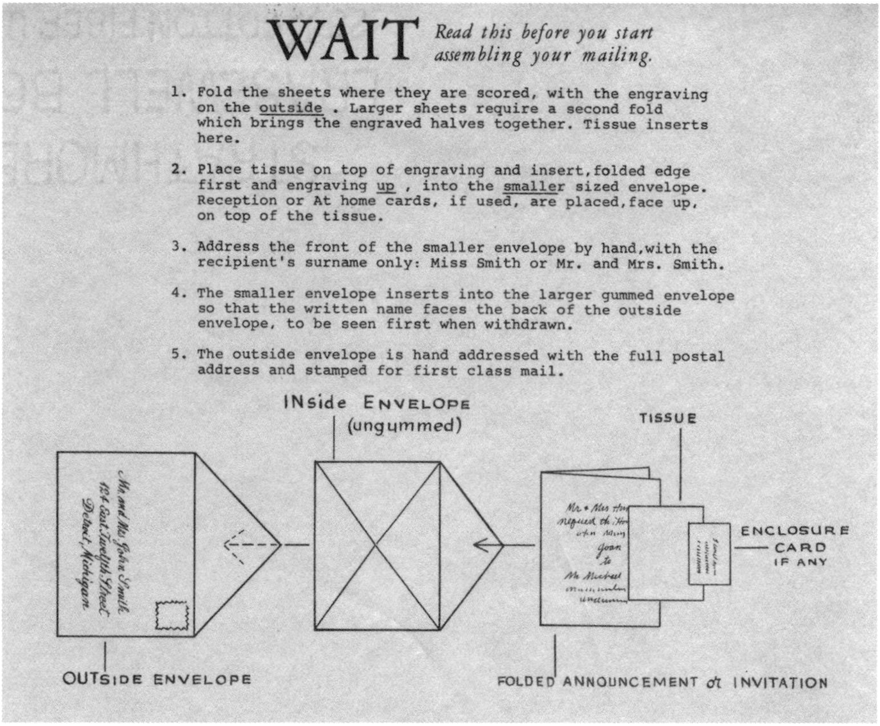

WAIT *Read this before you start assembling your mailing.*

1. Fold the sheets where they are scored, with the engraving on the outside . Larger sheets require a second fold which brings the engraved halves together. Tissue inserts here.
2. Place tissue on top of engraving and insert,folded edge first and engraving up , into the smaller sized envelope. Reception or At home cards, if used, are placed,face up, on top of the tissue.
3. Address the front of the smaller envelope by hand,with the recipient's surname only: Miss Smith or Mr. and Mrs. Smith.
4. The smaller envelope inserts into the larger gummed envelope so that the written name faces the back of the outside envelope, to be seen first when withdrawn.
5. The outside envelope is hand addressed with the full postal address and stamped for first class mail.

INside ENVELOPE
(ungummed)
TISSUE
Mr. and Mrs. John Smith
124 East Twelfth Street
Detroit, Michigan
ENCLOSURE
CARD
IF ANY
OUTSIDE ENVELOPE
FOLDED ANNOUNCEMENT or INVITATION

Fig. 14, opposite:
Letter sheet with hand-engraved cipher on hand-bordered onionskin with matching, hand-converted, fully lined onionskin envelope.
The sheet quarter-folds.
Engraved by Tommy Flax, New York, commissioned by the author, 2000.

Fig. 15:
Folding and assembling instructions for traditional wedding invitation suite.
Lehman Brothers Inc., New Haven, Connecticut, before 1980s.

Fig. 16:
Onionskin letter sheets, folded, with matching, hand-converted, fully lined onionskin envelope. The sheet quarter-folds.
Commissioned by the author, New York, 2001.

THE WRITING OF A PERSONAL NOTE OR LETTER

1. PREPARE A PLACE IN WHICH TO WRITE. IT IS VERY IMPORTANT THAT THIS BE A QUIET PLACE, ONE WHERE YOU WILL TEMPORARILY BE LEFT ALONE. ROMANTICS LIKE HIGH, VAULTED CEILINGS; PRAGMATICS LIKE LOW-SLUNG HUTS. SOME PEOPLE REQUIRE BIG GOTHIC WINDOWS FILLED WITH SUNLIGHT; OTHERS REQUIRE CANDLELIGHT AND BED.
2. PREFERABLY, YOUR PLACE SHOULD BE AWAY FROM ELECTRONIC MEDIA: NO PHONES, BLACKBERRYS, RADIOS, STEREOS (ALTHOUGH SOME QUIET CLASSICAL MUSIC IS OKAY). ESPECIALLY THIS MEANS GETTING AWAY FROM TELEVISIONS, DVD PLAYERS, AND COMPUTERS OF ANY KIND.
3. IF THE PLACE IS NOT A DESIGNATED WRITING AREA AND USED ONLY INTERMITTENTLY FOR THIS PURPOSE, BE SURE TO CLEAR A SPACE AT LEAST AS WIDE AS YOUR ARM SPAN. CLEAN THE SURFACE. SELECT A COMFORTABLE CHAIR. ARRANGE YOUR WRITING SUPPLIES. (THE RIGHT ENVIRONMENT WILL PUT YOU IN THE PROPER FRAME OF MIND. JUST AS A GREAT NOVEL OR EXCELLENT PLAY OR RESTAURANT MEAL TRANSFORMS, YOU WILL IMMEDIATELY BE ABLE TO FOCUS ON YOUR OWN THOUGHTS.)
4. WASH YOUR HANDS. RETURN TO THE WRITING SPACE AND SIT DOWN IN THE CHAIR. ALIGN YOUR FEET DIRECTLY BENEATH YOUR KNEES, YOUR FEET FACING RELATIVELY FORWARD. LET YOUR HANDS FALL NATURALLY TO YOUR SIDES. RELAX YOUR HEAD, NECK, AND SHOULDERS, INHALE DEEPLY, AND LET GRAVITY GENTLY PULL YOUR HEAD FORWARD. TAKE FIVE TO TEN DELIBERATE BREATHS WHILE LOOKING DOWNWARD AT

NOTHING IN PARTICULAR. CLEAR YOUR MIND. HUM SOFTLY IF YOU NEED TO. NOW PLACE YOUR HANDS ON THE WORK SURFACE. IF YOUR MIND HAS CLEARED AND YOU FEEL CALM, LIFT YOUR GAZE AND BEGIN. (WARNING: AT NO TIME IS IT ADVISABLE TO ENTER INTO THE ACT OF PERSONAL CORRESPONDENCE RASHLY OR IN AN AGITATED STATE UNLESS YOU ARE PASSIONATELY IN LOVE OR ABOUT TO FOUND A NEW NATION AND ARE VERY SURE OF THIS LOVE OR THE VICTORY OF THIS NEW NATION. OTHERWISE I URGE YOU TO TRY THE EXERCISE AGAIN.)

5. TAKE A SHEET OF WRITING PAPER (NOTE CARD FOR BRIEF OR EMPHATIC MESSAGES, CORRESPONDENCE CARDS FOR SOMETHING A TAD MORE INVOLVED, LETTER SHEET FOR WORTHWHILE DISCUSSIONS). SELECT YOUR FAVORITE WRITING INSTRUMENT AND BEGIN TO WRITE. WHEN CONSCIENTIOUSLY APPLIED, THE ABOVE STEPS SHOULD ALLOW YOUR WORDS TO FLOW.
6. READ THE CORRESPONDENCE WHEN DONE. IF CHANGES OR CORRECTIONS ARE REQUIRED, REWRITE YOUR NOTE OR LETTER ON A NEW PIECE OF STATIONERY RATHER THAN CROSSING OUT OR ADDING WORDS. KEEP AN EARLY DRAFT FOR YOUR RECORDS. PLACE THE COMPLETED DOCUMENT IN ITS ENVELOPE SO THAT IT FACES YOU WHEN OPENED FROM THE BACK. SEAL THE ENVELOPE FOR POSTING. TUCK THE BACK FLAP IN OR LIGHTLY TACK THE ADHESIVE IF HAND DELIVERED.
7. REPLACE MATERIALS, PUT CORRESPONDENCE IN A CONSPICUOUS PLACE FOR POSTING OR DELIVERY, REPLACE THE CHAIR UPON WHICH YOU SAT.

without a monogram or contact information but sometimes include a simple name or adornment. If a watermark is present, it should be right reading (i.e., reading the same way as the text). Monarch sheets are folded twice, into thirds, to fit inside a monarch envelope.

Note card, flat: Besides commercial, preprinted greeting cards, flat note cards (one-piece cards without folds) are the most popular stationery item used today. Traditionally, they were considered the domain of gentlemen: the fact that there is only one piece of paper requires brevity and a brisk, firm tone. Flat note cards may be written on the front and the back.

A monogram or one-line name, appropriately engraved, often appears centered at the top of a flat note. It is just as appropriate, though, for a family crest, or monogram, to be engraved in the upper right or left corner. Historically, flat cards were always oriented horizontally, but today's note cards can be vertical as well. As with a calling card, there is a tradition to strike through the engraved name and sign with a more familiar and personal moniker if you want to let the recipient know that you are more than formal acquaintances. [**Fig. 17**]

Note card, folded: The folded note card offers a bit of privacy, as the front only provides space for an engraving, while the message is discreetly contained within the interior. The proper way to write on a folded note card is to start on the inside right panel, continue on the inside left, and complete on the back. One never commences the message on the front of the card.

Mourning stationery: Mourning stationery was essential in the nineteenth-century communication toolbox and may have reached its apogee in the Victorian era. In those days, grieving women wore heavy black veils to separate them from the public. Most cultures allowed for this outward sign of grieving, but many of these traditions have been lost and these days it's expected we just "get on" with our lives.

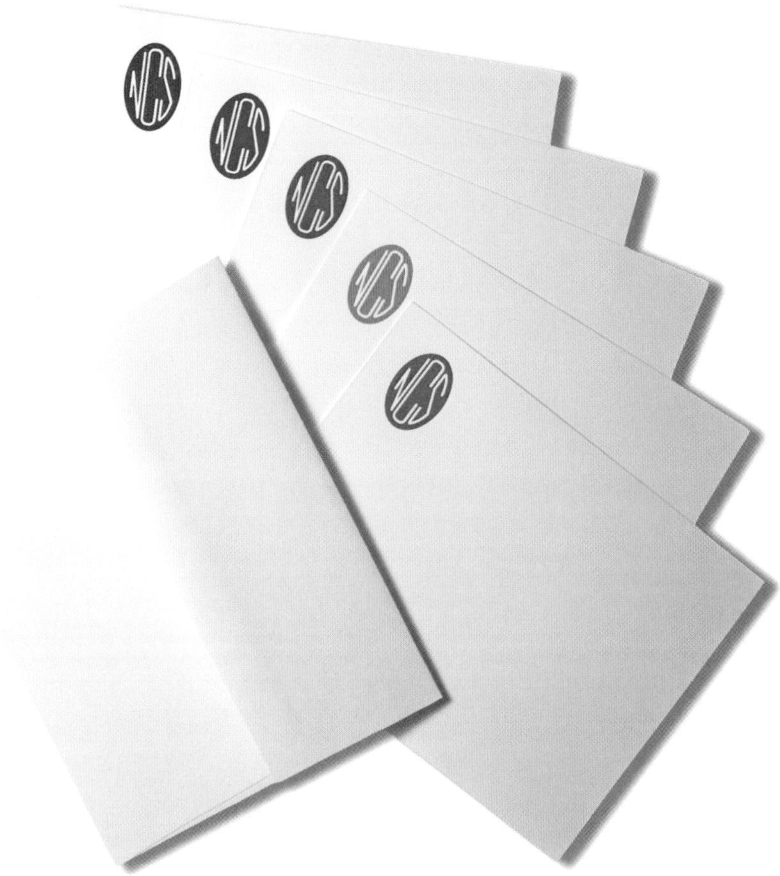
NCS
NCS
NCS
NCS
NCS

Fig. 17:
One of the author's many monograms and ciphers, photoengraved in five different colors on flat white note cards.

QUESTION

When is it appropriate to send a thank-you note?

ANSWER

A THANK-YOU NOTE IS ALWAYS APPROPRIATE. ANY ACT OF THOUGHTFULNESS, KINDNESS, OR RECOGNITION SHOULD BE RECIPROCATED PROMPTLY WITH A HANDWRITTEN NOTE.

IT IS IMPROPER TO USE A CARD WITH A PREPRINTED "THANK YOU" AS A FOLLOW-UP TO AN EMPLOYMENT INTERVIEW. INSTEAD USE A PLAIN, FOLDED NOTE OR A FLAT CARD ON WHICH JUST YOUR NAME IS PRINTED OR ENGRAVED. IT IS ALSO APPROPRIATE TO PRECEDE THE POSTED NOTE WITH A SHORT, POLITE E-MAIL THANKING THE INTERVIEWER FOR HIS OR HER TIME AND SHARING YOUR ENTHUSIASM FOR THE JOB.

This does not allow for the natural process of healing nor any gracious way of dealing with profound emotions. Mourning stationery, with its distinctive black border on each item, functioned as a visual signal that the sender was grieving the death of someone close to him or her. Traditionally, the various stages of mourning were indicated by the width of the black border, which diminished with time.[9] [**Figs. 18, 19**] As with many traditions of engraved social stationery, this protocol is a formal reminder that we should still honor and respect each specific passage in the cycle of life. [**Figs. 20, 21**]

CONDOLENCE LETTER

A LETTER OF CONDOLENCE SHOULD BE WRITTEN BY HAND WITH A BLACK OR DARK BLUE INK PEN. A SMALL NOTE SHEET, FOLDED IN HALF, IS BEST. ONE SIDE OF THE SHEET IS ALL THAT IS REQUIRED, AND THE LENGTH IS DETERMINED BY HOW INTIMATE YOU ARE WITH THE RECENTLY DECEASED AND THE PERSON TO WHOM YOU ARE ADDRESSING THE LETTER. IF YOU MUST PURCHASE A PREPRINTED CARD, ADD YOUR OWN MESSAGE. WRITE AS YOU WOULD SPEAK TO THE PERSON IN COMPANY, IN YOUR OWN VOICE. A FEW GUIDELINES:

– MENTION THAT YOU ARE SORRY FOR HIS OR HER LOSS, AND INCLUDE THE NAME OF THE DECEASED AND THE NATURE OF YOUR RELATIONSHIP.
– MENTION SOMETHING SPECIAL ABOUT THE DECEASED, PERHAPS A SPECIFIC TIME THAT YOU SHARED WITH THE RECIPIENT AND DECEASED.
– IF APPROPRIATE, FIGURE OUT A WAY THAT YOU MIGHT HELP THE SURVIVOR WITH SOME DOMESTIC OR PROFESSIONAL DUTY. MAKE IT A SINCERE AND DIRECT OFFER, AND MAKE SURE THAT IT CAN BE FULFILLED.
– CLOSE THE LETTER WITH AN OFFER OF SYMPATHY. BE BRIEF. WHILE A RESPONSE IS SOCIALLY EXPECTED, IT IS NOT NECESSARY THAT THE BEREAVED ANSWER EACH AND EVERY SYMPATHY CORRESPONDENCE.

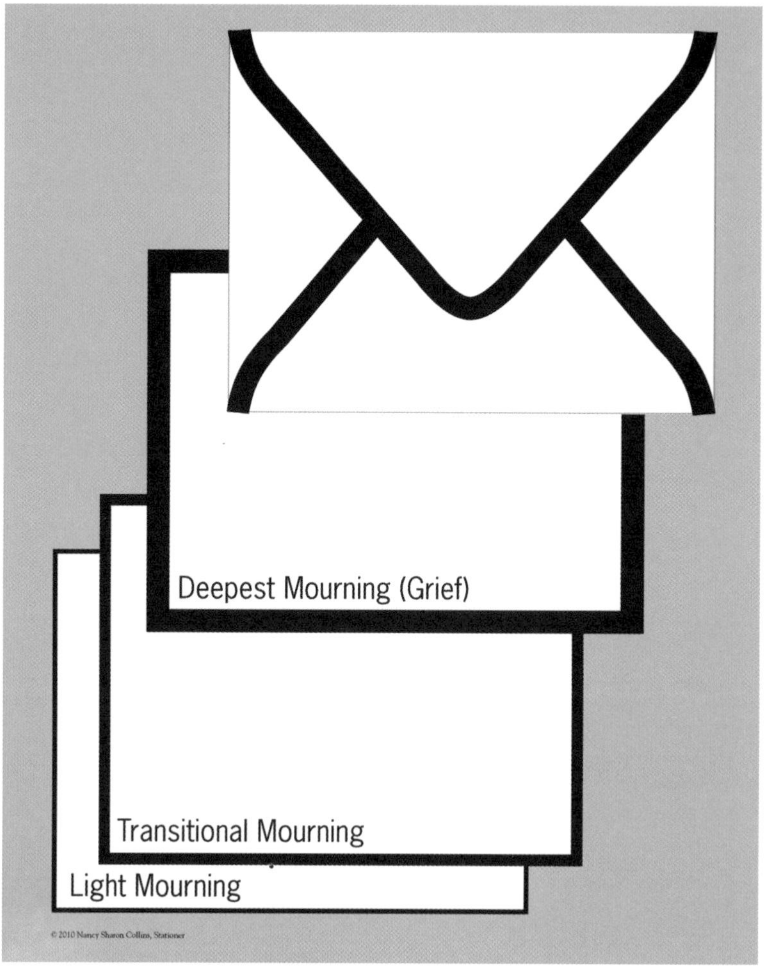
Deepest Mourning (Grief)
Transitional Mourning
Light Mourning
© 2010 Nancy Sharon Collins, Stationer

Fig. 18, above:
Diagram showing the various stages of mourning as indicated by the varying widths of the stationery border. The envelope would also be bordered to match the particular stage of grief. The envelope shown here, with the widest border, would have been used in the early stages of grief.

Fig. 19, opposite, top:
Photoengraved initial from a hand-engraved die on contemporary mourning stationery note cards.
Created by the author, 2010.

Fig. 20, opposite, bottom:
Monument-unveiling card from figure 21.

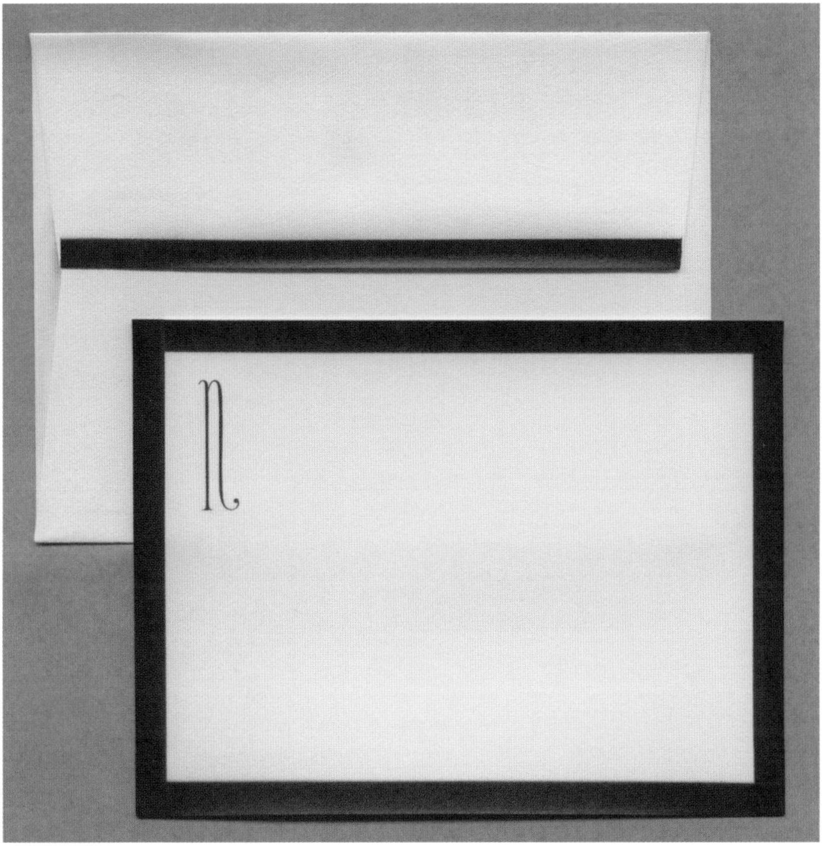

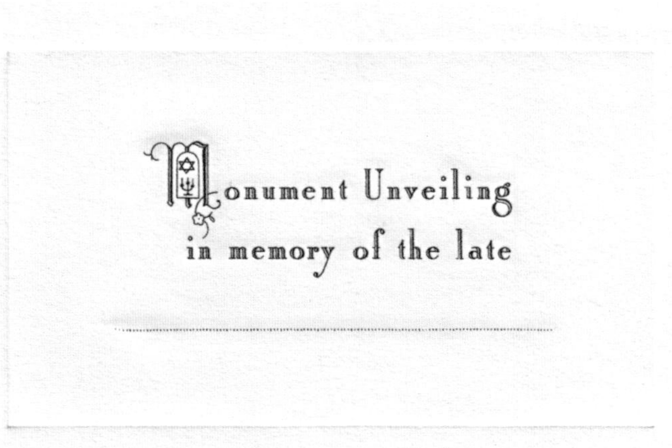
Monument Unveiling
in memory of the late

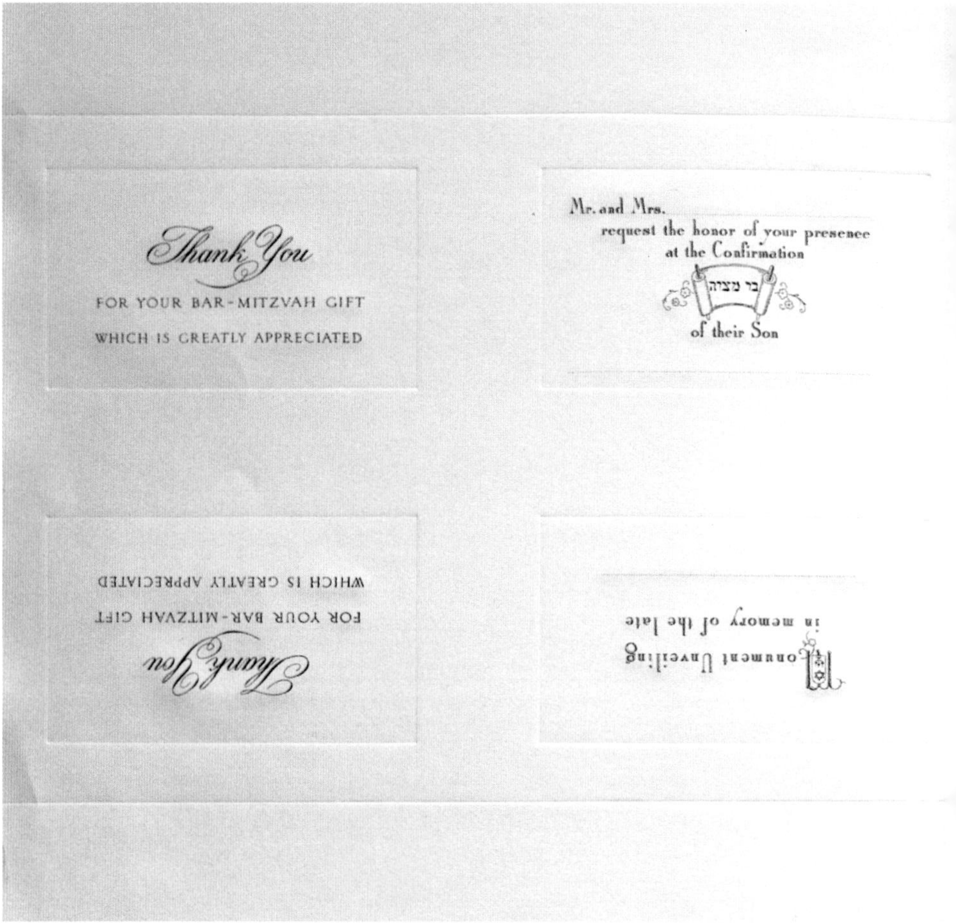
Thank You
FOR YOUR BAR-MITZVAH GIFT
WHICH IS GREATLY APPRECIATED
Mr. and Mrs.
request the honor of your presence
at the Confirmation
of their Son

Fig. 21:
Uncut sheet of cards including condolence, circumcision, confirmation, and bar mitzvah notices and invitations. Multiple items are printed on one sheet because it is more cost-effective to do one makeready and press run than separate ones for each different piece.
Engraved by Lehman Brothers Inc., New Haven, Connecticut.

Mr. and Mrs.
request the honor of your presence
at the Circumcision
ברית מילה
of their Son
Mr. and Mrs.
request the honor of your presence
at the Circumcision (ברית מילה)
of their son
You are cordially invited to attend the
פדיון הבן
(Pidyon Haben)
of our Son
Mr. and Mrs.
request the honor of your presence
at the Confirmation (בר מצוה)
of their son

Chapter Four

BUSINESS CORRESPONDENCE

The origins of contemporary business cards, identity systems, brochures, ads, and other marketing vehicles can be found in the late-1700s trade card. [**Figs. 1–3**] These advertised the services and goods offered by shops, differentiated the business from its competitors, and functioned as a wayfinding device (with written directions or a map) through streets and alleyways prior to the invention of numbered building addresses. A lot of information was expected from one little card.

The trade card evolved into the billhead, used for business letters, estimates, invoices, and receipts of delivery, which eventually evolved into the corporate letterhead. Early billheads and trade cards were engraved from copperplates. As billheads developed, more and more elaborate visualizations of information, company specialization, and advertising appeared at the top of the page. With the rise of industrialization in the United States, it became typical for pictorial renditions of idealized manufacturing plants to be engraved and lithographed at the head of business correspondence. [**Figs. 4, 5**] Sometimes the same image of a factory was used for multiple locations.

As commercial printing processes became more advanced during the 1800s, the possibilities for using ornamental patterns, decorative borders, and other embellishments became increasingly varied and elaborate. Perhaps to differentiate from the vulgar masses of commercial shopkeepers and manufacturers, professional offices relied on engraved letterheads as their preferred form of business stationery. Across America, engraved letterheads and business cards came to be expected of doctors, lawyers, and anyone wanting to appear serious and knowledgeable. [**Fig. 6**] Over the centuries, many styles for engraved letterheads developed, running the gamut from the sober to the eccentric. [**Figs. 7–12**]

Today standard practice for many start-up businesses is still to create a logo, business card, and letterhead, but such items of stationery are usually printed by offset lithography or digitally rather than engraved. In an age when social media has become so important,

CHARLES PEATY,
Estate & House Agent, Auctioneer & Appraiser,
UPHOLSTERER, UNDERTAKER, &c,
64 High Street, Southampton.
Yachts fitted out.

Edward Low
BREAD & BISCUIT BAKER,
& Cornchandler,
Opposite Hollywood Brewhouse,
LITTLE CHELSEA.

John A. Lowell
Arthur S. Doane
John A. Lowell & Co....
Engravers and Art Publishers
Mason Building
70 Kilby St
BOSTON

Fig. 1, top:
Engraved trade card. Note the small advertisement for a house to let to the left of the white building. W. Jones, London, eighteenth century.
Collection of Richard D. Sheaff.

Fig. 2, middle:
Engraved trade card. This engraver's proof is printed on pinkish paper stock. Edward Low. Bread & Biscuit Baker, & Cornhandler (English, date unknown).
Collection of Richard D. Sheaff.

Fig. 3, bottom:
Engraved trade card advertising the virtuosity of John A. Lowell & Co., Boston, 1880s–1920s.
Collection of Richard D. Sheaff.

it is interesting to note that the letterhead remains relevant as well. Recently, there has been a rise in the use of engraved letterhead and business cards among young and very hip upstarts. [**Figs. 13–15**]

FISCHER LIME AND CEMENT CO.
INCORPORATED
BUILDING MATERIALS
PHONE 8-0211
L. D. PHONE 379
WALNUT ST. LINDEN TO PONTOTOC
MEMPHIS, TENN.
January 12 1942

BELKNAP HARDWARE & MANUFACTURING CO.
ESTABLISHED 1840
INCORPORATED 1880
111 EAST MAIN STREET ★ LOUISVILLE, KENTUCKY
August 31, 1942

Fig. 4, top:
Lithographed billhead styled after banknote engraving.
Publisher unknown, Memphis, Tennessee, 1942.

Fig. 5, bottom:
Lithographed billhead styled after banknote engraving.
Publisher unknown, Louisville, Kentucky, 1942.

Fig. 6, right:
Engraved chart, with half-tone screens, depicting what is involved in the making of a letter, probably 1940s or early 1950s. At the time, offices commonly had secretaries on staff and sometimes even an entire stenographic pool dedicated solely to typing letters.
Strathmore Archives, Mohawk Fine Papers, Cohoes, New York.

Fig. 7, bottom left:
Classically folded business letterhead, monarch-size sheet, commercially engraved in two colors. Hart Engraving, Milwaukee, 1930s or 1940s.

Fig. 8, bottom right:
Offset lithography and engraved letterhead. Hart Engraving, Milwaukee, 1940s or 1950s.

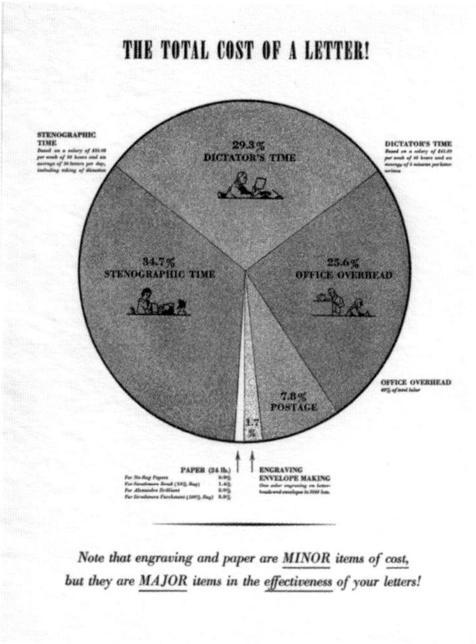
THE TOTAL COST OF A LETTER!
STENOGRAPHIC TIME
29.3% DICTATOR'S TIME
DICTATOR'S TIME
34.7% STENOGRAPHIC TIME
25.6% OFFICE OVERHEAD
OFFICE OVERHEAD
7.8% POSTAGE
1.7 %
PAPER (24 lb.)
ENGRAVING
ENVELOPE MAKING
Note that engraving and paper are MINOR items of cost,
but they are MAJOR items in the effectiveness of your letters!

Jack's Letter Service
Seventh Floor Brumder Building
Milwaukee, Wis.

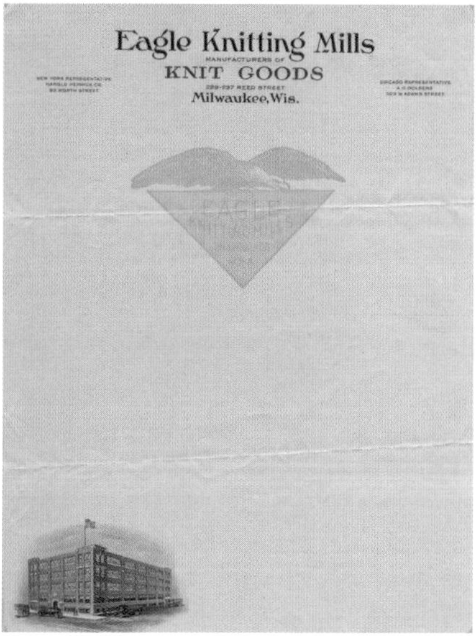
Eagle Knitting Mills
MANUFACTURERS OF
KNIT GOODS
Milwaukee, Wis.

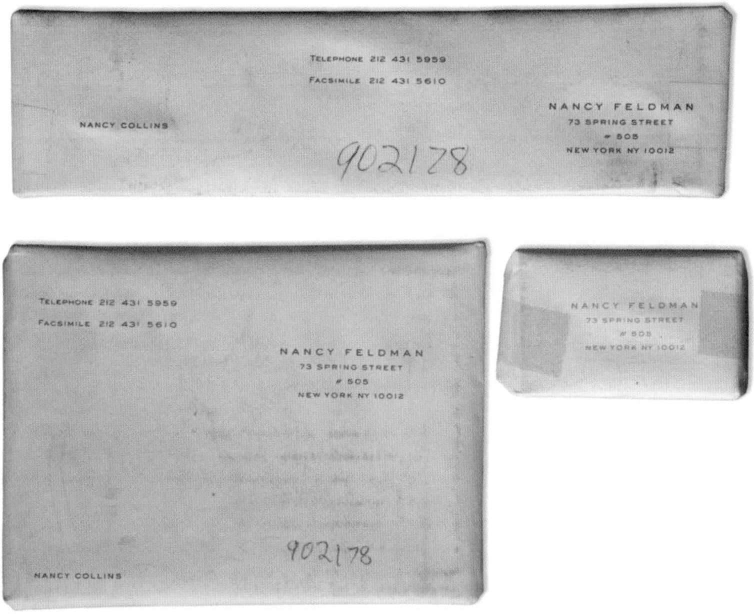
TELEPHONE 212 431 5959
FACSIMILE 212 431 5610
NANCY COLLINS
NANCY FELDMAN
73 SPRING STREET
505
NEW YORK NY 10012
902178
TELEPHONE 212 431 5959
FACSIMILE 212 431 5610
NANCY FELDMAN
73 SPRING STREET
505
NEW YORK NY 10012
902178
NANCY COLLINS
NANCY FELDMAN
73 SPRING STREET
505
NEW YORK NY 10012

TEXCRAFT STUDIOS
INCORPORATED
23 EAST 26TH STREET
NEW YORK CITY
These Examples of Matched Stationery
TEXCRAFT STUDIOS
BASIC DOLOMITE
PAPER
LETTER COST, ETC.

Fig. 9, top:
Letterhead, envelope, and business card dies, each wrapped in its press proof, engraved in Masterplate Style 2 Line Block (see page 175) and designed using a traditional professional letterhead for inspiration.
Artscroll, New York, commissioned by the author, 1986.

Fig. 10, bottom:
Example of an engraved set of business letterhead as displayed in a Strathmore Paper Company sample book.
Strathmore Archives, Mohawk Fine Papers, Cohoes, New York, probably 1940s or early 1950s.

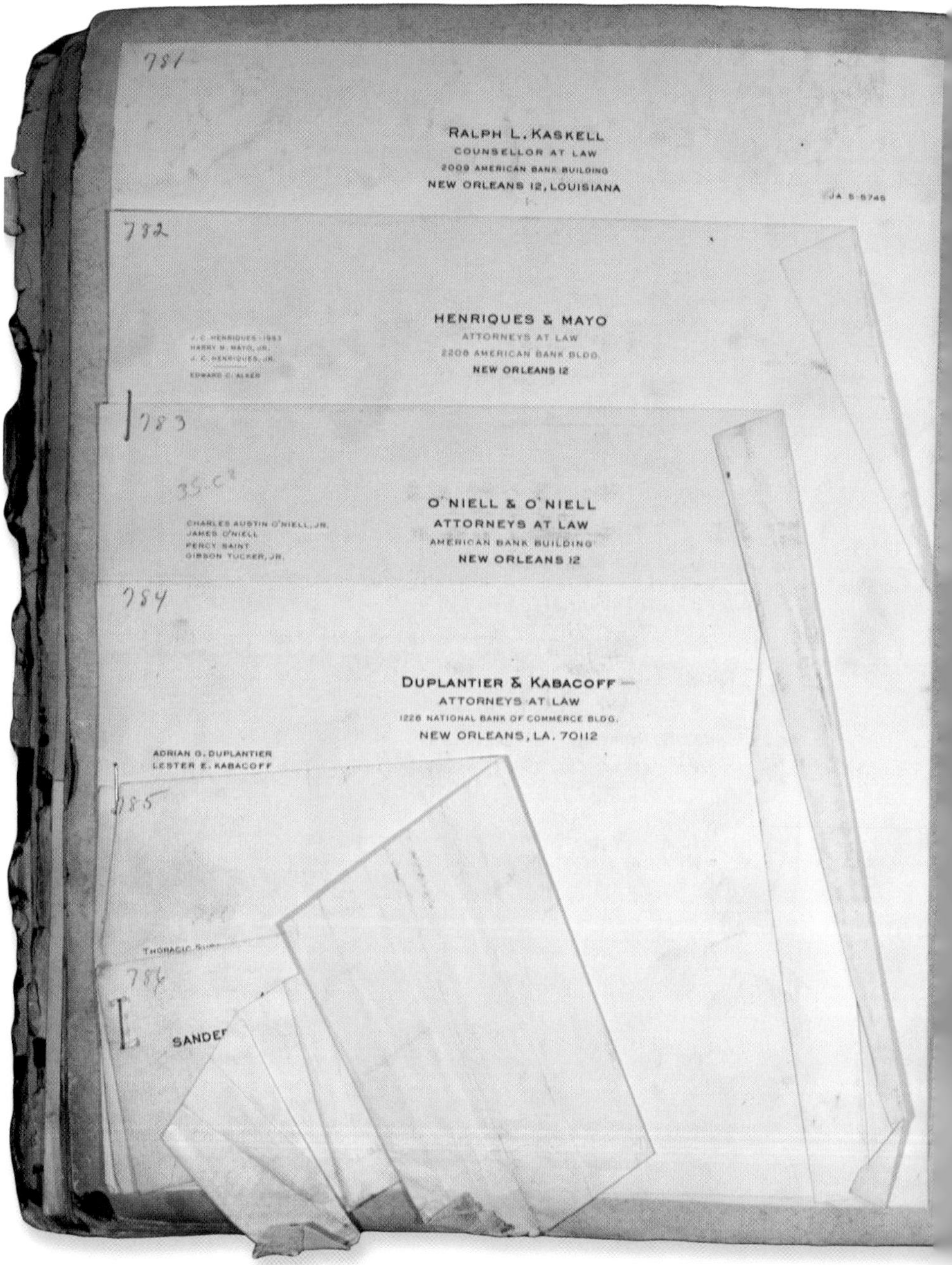
781
RALPH L. KASKELL
COUNSELLOR AT LAW
2009 AMERICAN BANK BUILDING
NEW ORLEANS 12, LOUISIANA
782
HENRIQUES & MAYO
ATTORNEYS AT LAW
2208 AMERICAN BANK BLDG.
NEW ORLEANS 12
783
O'NIELL & O'NIELL
ATTORNEYS AT LAW
AMERICAN BANK BUILDING
NEW ORLEANS 12
CHARLES AUSTIN O'NIELL, JR.
JAMES O'NIELL
PERCY SAINT
GIBSON TUCKER, JR.
784
DUPLANTIER & KABACOFF
ATTORNEYS AT LAW
1228 NATIONAL BANK OF COMMERCE BLDG.
NEW ORLEANS, LA. 70112
ADRIAN G. DUPLANTIER
LESTER E. KABACOFF

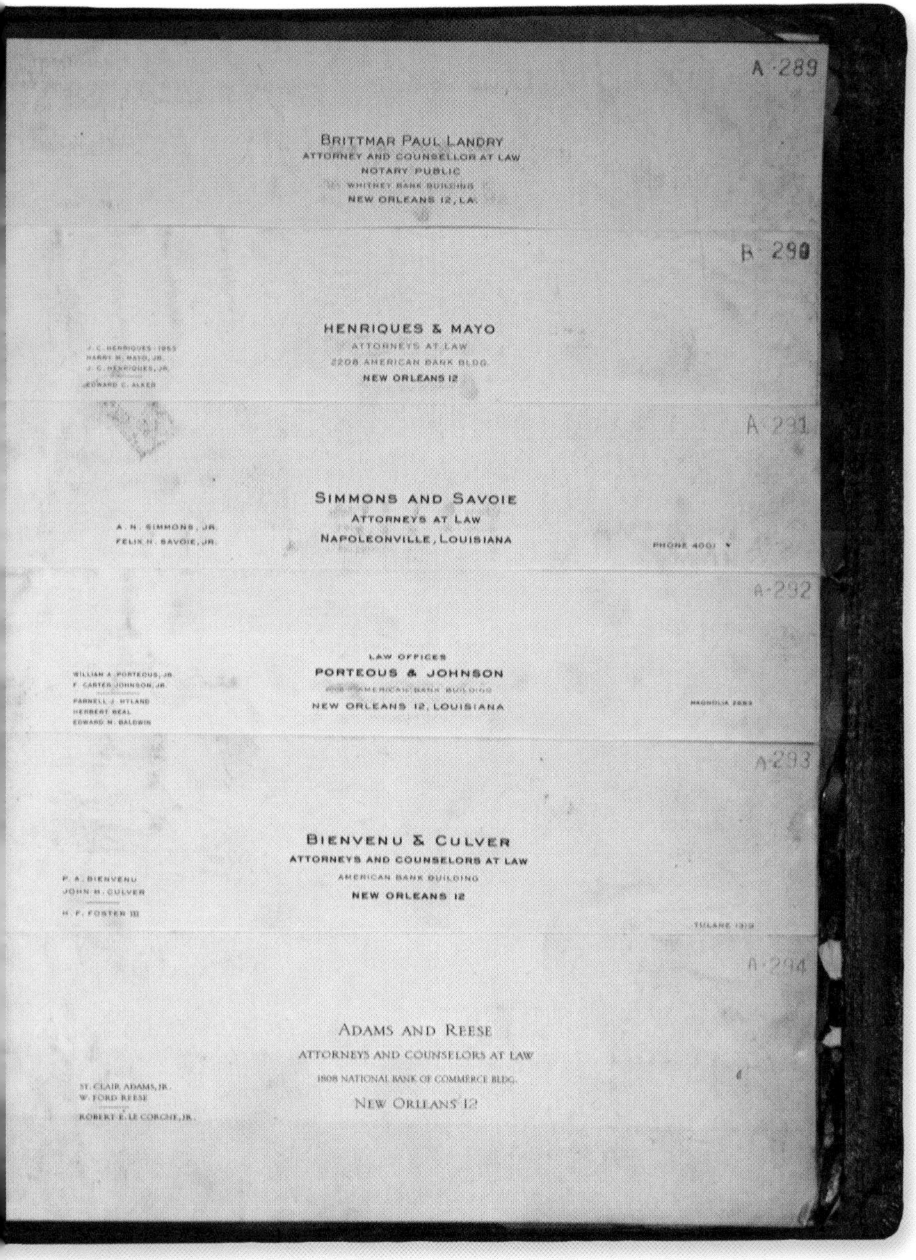
A-289
BRITTMAR PAUL LANDRY
ATTORNEY AND COUNSELLOR AT LAW
NOTARY PUBLIC
WHITNEY BANK BUILDING
NEW ORLEANS 12, LA.
B 290
HENRIQUES & MAYO
ATTORNEYS AT LAW
2208 AMERICAN BANK BLDG.
NEW ORLEANS 12
A-291
SIMMONS AND SAVOIE
ATTORNEYS AT LAW
NAPOLEONVILLE, LOUISIANA
A. N. SIMMONS, JR.
FELIX H. SAVOIE, JR.
PHONE 4001
A-292
LAW OFFICES
PORTEOUS & JOHNSON
AMERICAN BANK BUILDING
NEW ORLEANS 12, LOUISIANA
A-293
BIENVENU & CULVER
ATTORNEYS AND COUNSELORS AT LAW
AMERICAN BANK BUILDING
NEW ORLEANS 12
F. A. BIENVENU
JOHN M. CULVER
H. F. FOSTER III
A-294
ADAMS AND REESE
ATTORNEYS AND COUNSELORS AT LAW
1808 NATIONAL BANK OF COMMERCE BLDG.
NEW ORLEANS 12
ST. CLAIR ADAMS, JR.
W. FORD REESE
ROBERT E. LE CORGNE, JR.

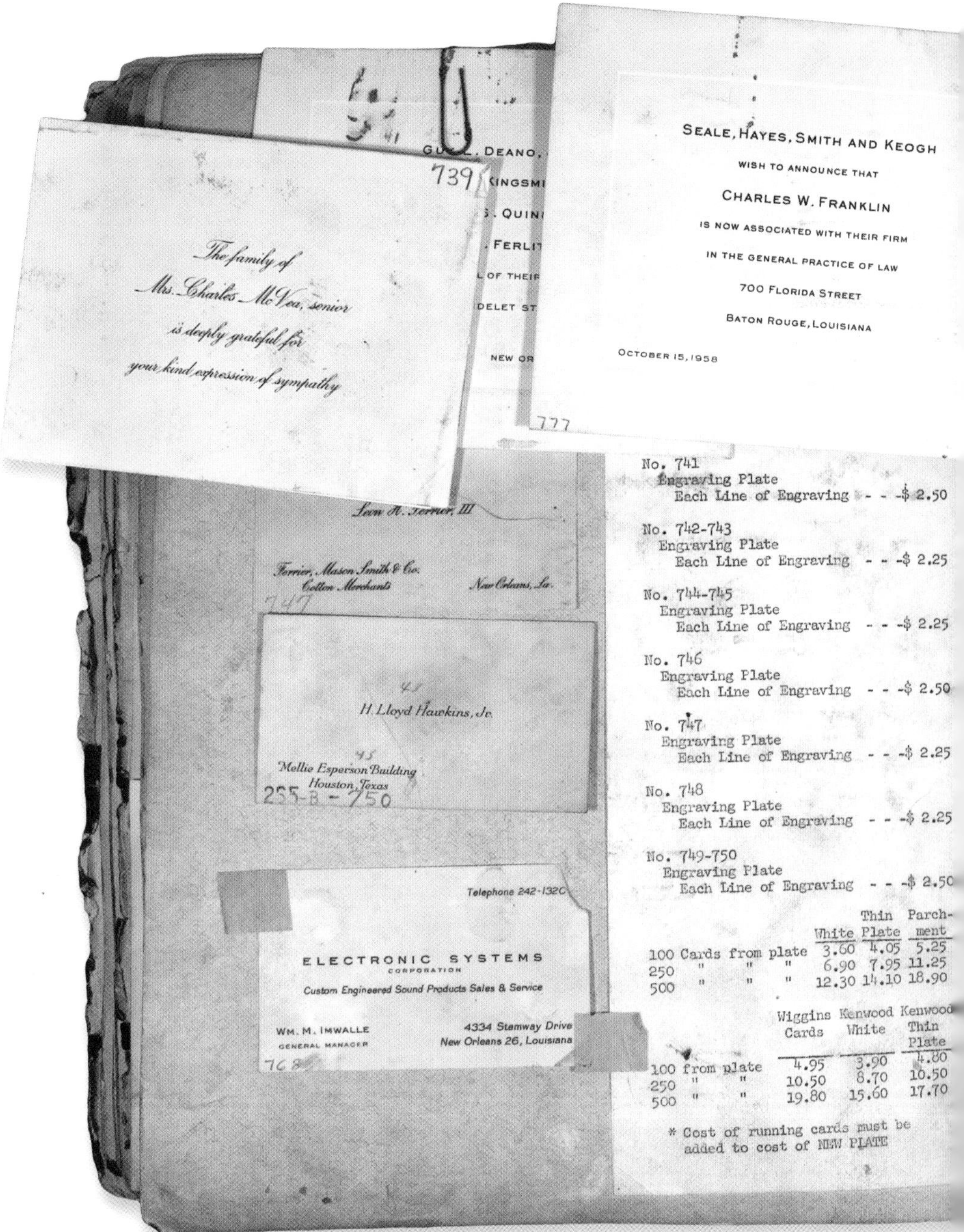
SEALE, HAYES, SMITH AND KEOGH
WISH TO ANNOUNCE THAT
CHARLES W. FRANKLIN
IS NOW ASSOCIATED WITH THEIR FIRM
IN THE GENERAL PRACTICE OF LAW
700 FLORIDA STREET
BATON ROUGE, LOUISIANA
OCTOBER 15, 1958
777
739
The family of
Mrs. Charles McVea, senior
is deeply grateful for
your kind expression of sympathy
Leon H. Ferrier, III
Ferrier, Mason Smith & Co.
Cotton Merchants
New Orleans, La.
747
H. Lloyd Hawkins, Jr.
Mellie Esperson Building
Houston, Texas
255-B - 750
Telephone 242-132C
ELECTRONIC SYSTEMS
CORPORATION
Custom Engineered Sound Products Sales & Service
WM. M. IMWALLE
GENERAL MANAGER
4334 Stemway Drive
New Orleans 26, Louisiana
768
No. 741
Engraving Plate
Each Line of Engraving - - -$ 2.50
No. 742-743
Engraving Plate
Each Line of Engraving - - -$ 2.25
No. 744-745
Engraving Plate
Each Line of Engraving - - -$ 2.25
No. 746
Engraving Plate
Each Line of Engraving - - -$ 2.50
No. 747
Engraving Plate
Each Line of Engraving - - -$ 2.25
No. 748
Engraving Plate
Each Line of Engraving - - -$ 2.25
No. 749-750
Engraving Plate
Each Line of Engraving - - -$ 2.50
White Thin Plate Parchment
100 Cards from plate 3.60 4.05 5.25
250 " " " 6.90 7.95 11.25
500 " " " 12.30 14.10 18.90
Wiggins Cards Kenwood White Kenwood Thin Plate
100 from plate 4.95 3.90 4.80
250 " " 10.50 8.70 10.50
500 " " 19.80 15.60 17.70
* Cost of running cards must be
added to cost of NEW PLATE

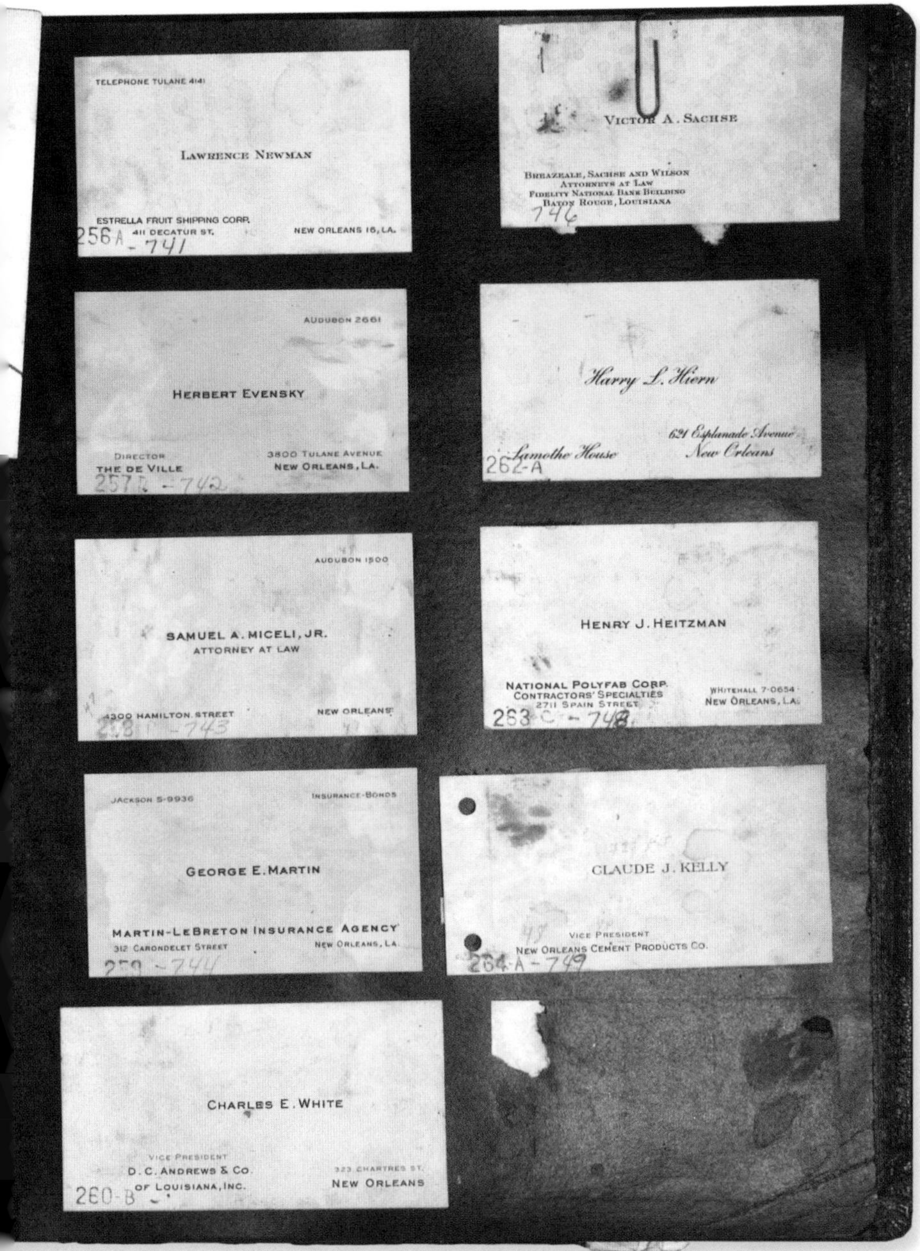
TELEPHONE TULANE 4141
LAWRENCE NEWMAN
ESTRELLA FRUIT SHIPPING CORP.
411 DECATUR ST.
NEW ORLEANS 16, LA.
256 A - 741
VICTOR A. SACHSE
BREAZEALE, SACHSE AND WILSON
ATTORNEYS AT LAW
FIDELITY NATIONAL BANK BUILDING
BATON ROUGE, LOUISIANA
746
AUDUBON 2661
HERBERT EVENSKY
DIRECTOR
THE DE VILLE
3800 TULANE AVENUE
NEW ORLEANS, LA.
- 742
Harry L. Hiern
621 Esplanade Avenue
New Orleans
Lamothe House
262-A
AUDUBON 1500
SAMUEL A. MICELI, JR.
ATTORNEY AT LAW
4300 HAMILTON STREET
NEW ORLEANS
- 743
HENRY J. HEITZMAN
NATIONAL POLYFAB CORP.
CONTRACTORS' SPECIALTIES
2711 SPAIN STREET
WHITEHALL 7-0654
NEW ORLEANS, LA.
263 C - 748
JACKSON 5-9936
INSURANCE-BONDS
GEORGE E. MARTIN
MARTIN-LEBRETON INSURANCE AGENCY
312 CARONDELET STREET
NEW ORLEANS, LA.
- 744
CLAUDE J. KELLY
VICE PRESIDENT
NEW ORLEANS CEMENT PRODUCTS CO.
264-A - 749
CHARLES E. WHITE
VICE PRESIDENT
D. C. ANDREWS & CO.
OF LOUISIANA, INC.
323 CHARTRES ST.
NEW ORLEANS
260-B

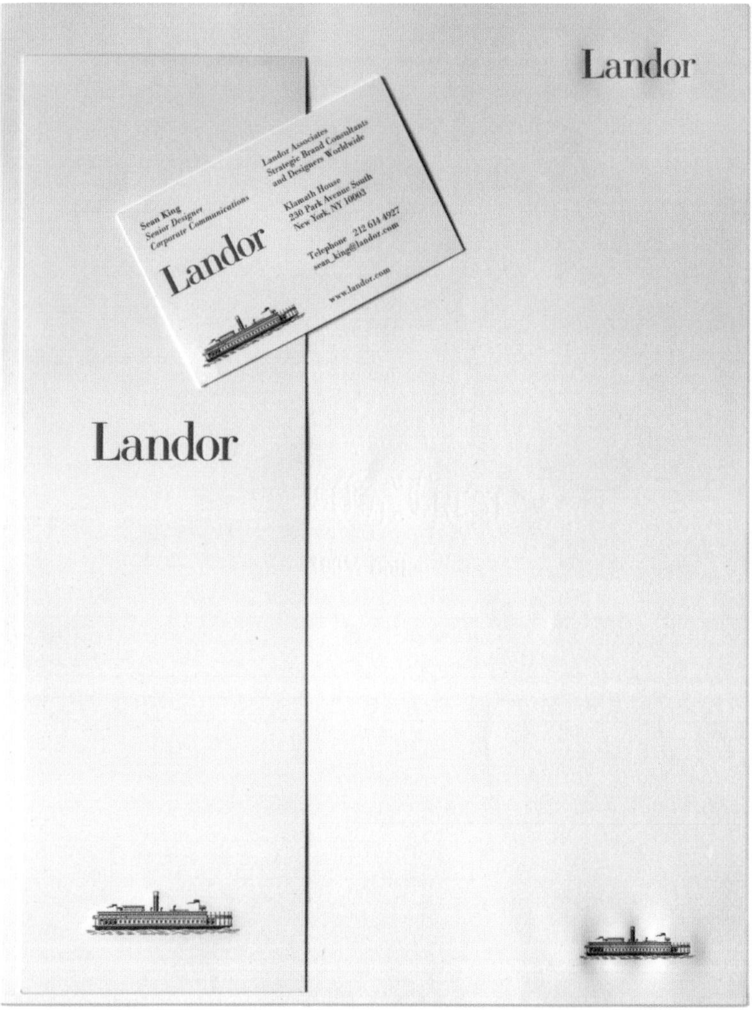
Landor
Landor
Landor
Sean King
Senior Designer
Corporate Communications
Landor Associates
Strategic Brand Consultants
and Designers Worldwide
Klamath House
230 Park Avenue South
New York, NY 10003
Telephone 212 614 4927
sean_king@landor.com
www.landor.com

Fig. 11, pages 104–105: Samples of engraved business letterheads.
Lehman Brothers Inc., New Haven, Connecticut, ca. 1930s–1970s.

Fig. 12, pages 106–107: Examples of business stationery from a sample book of engraved stationery items, ca. 1930s–1970s.
Lehman Brothers Inc., New Haven, Connecticut.

Fig. 13, above: Letterhead, business card, and with compliments card for Landor Associates. Landor discontinued use of engraving for its own branding in 2007.
The Ligature, Los Angeles, commissioned by Landor, pre-2007.

Ben Friedman
Partner
ben@iconologic.com
+1 404 260 4502 office
+1 404 822 5035 mobile
40 Inwood Circle NE
Atlanta, GA, USA 30309
www.iconologic.com
Roger Black Studio Inc.
245 Fifth Avenue
Suite 2345
New York, NY 10016
info@rogerblack.com
+1·212·481·9800
Fax: +1·646·651·4455
http://rogerblack.com
TypoBRAND
MARK VAN BRONKHORST
mvb@typobrand.com
TYPOBRAND LLC
1019 Pomona Avenue
Albany CA 94706 USA
510 525 4288 TELEPHONE
510 525 4289 FACSIMILE
TypoBrand.com

Fig. 14, top:
Three contemporary engraved business cards from members of the graphic design and typography communities.

Fig. 15, bottom:
Detail of letterhead, winner of 2007 Cronite Cup, commercial engraving in nine colors. (Viewed at the proper angle, the spear pierces the head of Jesus.)
Grabados Fernando Fernandez, Mexico City, 2007.

Chapter Five

CIPHERS AND MONOGRAMS, FAMILY CRESTS AND SEALS

During the Victorian era, unique combinations of letters in the form of ciphers and monograms became popular elements to engrave on stationery. A cipher is any arrangement of initials used together in one design (like a logo) [**Figs. 1–3**], while the letters of a monogram share essential strokes and curves, making it impossible to separate one letter from another.

Most monograms or ciphers used in stationery engraving come from a legacy of styles more than a century old. [**Figs. 4–6**] The tradition of paying homage to a previous generation's work by appropriating and modifying imagery for contemporary use is time honored and generally accepted. As a result, vintage sample sheets and monogram collections bound in albums can be used as inspiration. [**Figs. 7–14**]

FAMILY CRESTS, COATS OF ARMS, AND SEALS

> The newest thing in crests or monograms is to put them down at the bottom of the notepaper, instead of at the top as before, the chosen corner being the right-hand one. In case you have a lot of the old stock on hand, you turn the page upside down and apologise for the stupidity of the printer in a P.S.[1]
> —"Ladies Gossip," [Dunedin, New Zealand] *Otago Witness*, 1889

As a stationer, I am sometimes called upon to work with a family heirloom, usually to engrave a familial seal or crest for an invitation or upcoming function. A sweet gesture, this may be a nostalgic effort to rekindle family bonds or rebuild hereditary pride. [**Figs. 15–19**] While heraldic pageantry and devices are not my personal interest, I do enjoy working with any arcane piece of iconography, including family crests and seals. Americans have sought after crests and heraldic devices for centuries. For instance, the coat of arms shown in figures 20 to 22 was applied for by a U.S. citizen and granted by the British Crown.[2] [**Figs. 20–22**] It is not uncommon for emblems to be inspired by bits and pieces of history, borrowed from the old country, and repurposed for use in North America.[3]

The Victorian appetite for fancy goods and the genteel desire to associate with the rich and famous rivaled our current state of consumerism and penchant for notoriety. Crest and monogram collecting, a late nineteenth- and early twentieth-century pastime in Great Britain and, to some degree, the United States, is an example of this obsession. Crests, family seals, and monograms were saved in special albums similar to scrap- or stamp-collecting books, with decorative covers and preprinted pages, die-cut framings, and embossed motifs in which to paste specimens. Hobbyists focused on collecting interesting marks and seals from letters received. Coats of arms or monograms from famous families, politicians, opera stars, or members of the theater were particularly coveted and displayed. Some printing establishments sold packets of seals and ciphers—probably unauthorized—to customers, facilitating a collection's swift growth at relatively modest cost and popularizing the commission for such engravings.[4] [**Figs. 23–27**]

QUESTION

What is the difference between ciphers and monograms?

ANSWER

A CIPHER IS ANY ARRANGEMENT OF TWO OR MORE INITIALS. THE LETTERS DO NOT HAVE TO CONNECT. THE LETTERS OF A MONOGRAM, ON THE OTHER HAND, SHARE ESSENTIAL STROKES AND CURVES. MONOGRAMS DO NOT HAVE TO BE LEGIBLE, WHILE CIPHERS TYPICALLY ARE.

625 Irvington Avenue
Elizabeth, New Jersey
130 EAST END AVENUE
NEW YORK

Fig. 1, top:
Engraved cipher and lettering sample card. New York, ca. 1940s.

Fig. 2, left:
Cipher and hand-bordered note card, both in varnish-based ink, mid-twentieth century.

Fig. 3, right:
Hand-drawn, heavily ornamented cipher, in graphite pencil on tracing paper.
Noel Martin, Covington, Louisiana, 1970s–early 1990s.

DAMERON-PIERSON CO., LTD.

Figs. 4 (top), **5, 6** (following spread): These images show part of a collection of engraved monograms, ciphers, coat of arms, and club seals from the Jim Joly specialty printing company, New Orleans, which was flooded in the wake of Hurricane Katrina. The collection was donated to the Hill Memorial Library, Baton Rouge, Louisiana, in 2008. Most specimens are ½-inch-thick steel dies carefully wrapped in their original, engraved press proofs. As can be seen by the repetitious nature of some, monogram and cipher designs were recycled for different clients. It is interesting to compare some of these styles to those seen in figures 7, 8, and 9. Jim Joly Collection of Dameron-Pierson Co., Ltd. Steel Dies, Mss. 5071, Louisiana and Lower Mississippi Valley Collections, LSU Libraries.

M-1125
RC
DMC
SNB
CFJ
CAS
LJA
FWZ
MBH
AMG
MBA
BWM
MBB
GT
D
BEK
CCI
ID
HHB
BLE

EWE
VWC
FFH
SYC
SYC
CWC
FNS
MAW
AW
HBW
KFS
MBL
FGW
SVB
TWW
LVG
AMCo
KRF
MB
LUI
MTC
OBJ
CB+TCo
MTK
DHD

QUESTION

What do I do with my monogram when I get married?

ANSWER

USE IT. YOUR MONOGRAM REPRESENTS YOU, ALWAYS. EVEN IF YOU TAKE YOUR HUSBAND'S NAME, YOUR MONOGRAM IS THE MARK OF YOUR MOST PERSONAL SELF.

Fig. 7, opposite:
Sample sheet of Victorian, Edwardian, and early twentieth-century ciphers engraved in varnish-based ink, before 1970s.

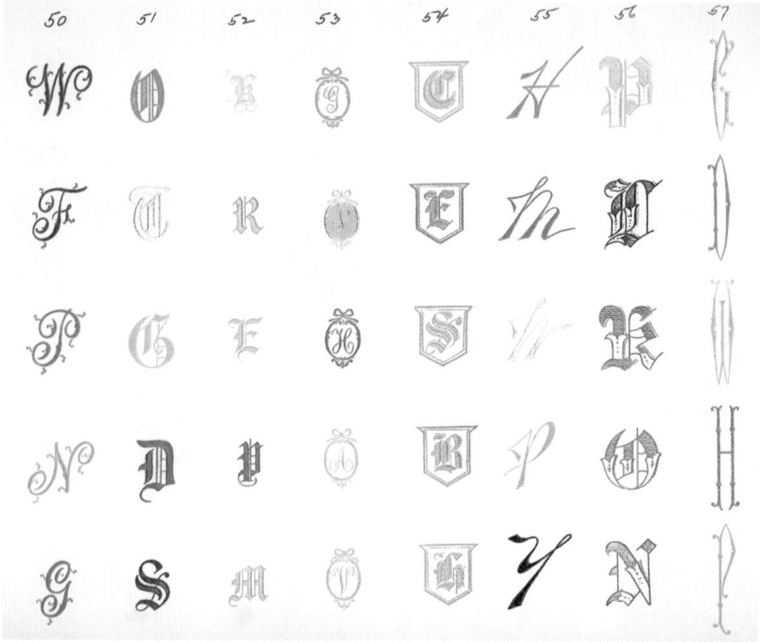

Fig. 8, top:
Sample sheet of decorative initials engraved in varnish-based ink, before 1970s. Styles include black letter (Old English), fancy script, Gothic, and initials enclosed within wreath and escutcheon (column 54).

Fig. 9, bottom:
Sample sheet of ciphers engraved in varnish-based ink, before 1970s. This is the original sample that inspired the ideas for the figures shown on page 133.

APR 2 1 2008

Fig. 10, top left:
Many of my own ciphers and monograms are inspired by older ones, and some of these go on to inspire the imaginations of my clients. This 2006 cipher is based on an earlier example in my personal collection. I drew various iterations on canary paper with a marker and graphite pencil, then cut and pasted the *n* from one sketch, the *s* from another, and the c from a third. Just like using layers in Adobe's Illustrator or Photoshop, drawing by tracing and compiling layers has the same wondrous characteristic of seeing through each layer until your design is just right. Then this layered art can be scanned into the computer. This image shows the original Sharpie marker drawing on tracing paper with canary paper overlay.

Fig. 11, top middle:
The original drawing overlay was scanned and the contrast increased to the appearance of absolute black and white, then turned into a bitmap file.

Fig. 12, top right,:
Press proof of ½-inch-thick steel die engraved according to the information provided in the bitmap file.
Engraved by Tommy Flax, New York, commissioned by the author, 2006.

Fig. 13, bottom left:
The die engraved from the digital drawing.
Commissioned by the author, New York, 2006.

Fig. 14, bottom right:
Cipher engraved on water-blue onionskin with matching onionskin envelope.

QUESTION

What is the difference between a family crest and a seal?

ANSWER

A CREST IS ONE ELEMENT IN A COAT OF ARMS, USUALLY AN ICON, SUCH AS A LION OR A STAG; BOTH ARE FROM THE HISTORIC EUROPEAN HERALDIC TRADITION. A SEAL IS USUALLY EMBOSSED, AND MAY SHARE ELEMENTS OF BUT IS NOT NECESSARILY RELATED TO HERALDRY.

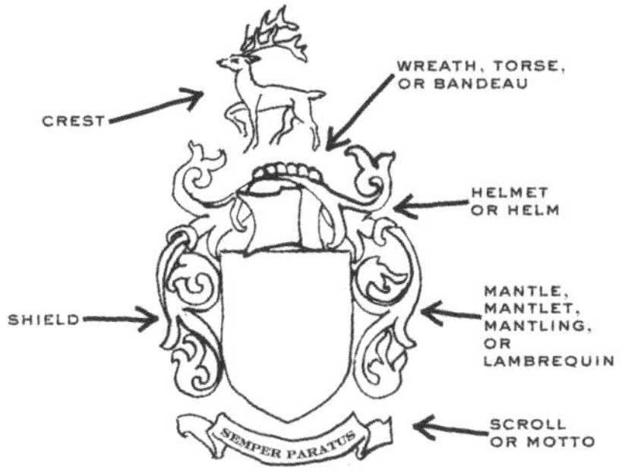
CREST
WREATH, TORSE, OR BANDEAU
HELMET OR HELM
SHIELD
MANTLE, MANTLET, MANTLING, OR LAMBREQUIN
SEMPER PARATUS
SCROLL OR MOTTO

H. M. QUEEN VICTORIA

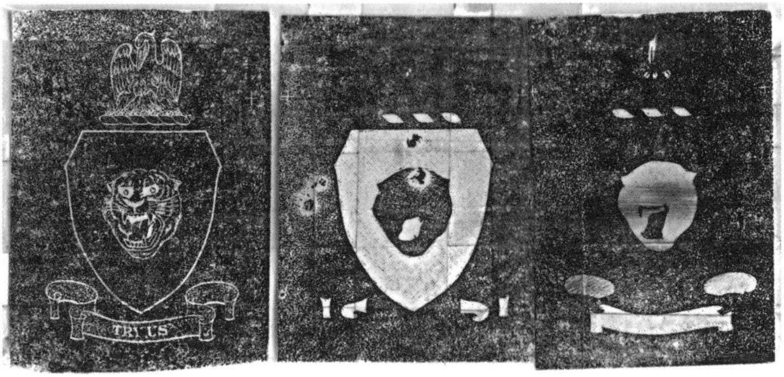

Fig. 15, top left:
Coat of arms diagram. The motto *semper paratus* translates to "always ready."

Fig. 16, top right:
Engraved coat of arms of H. M. Queen Victoria, measuring approximately one inch across. Monograms and seals such as this were sold in packets during the height of the Victorian album collecting craze.
William S. Lincoln, *The Lincoln Crest & Monogram Album*, 4th ed. (London: Lincoln, ca. 1880).

Fig. 17, bottom:
Relief prints from a three-color emblem consisting of three different dies. The emblem features a crest (pelican on top), shield (with tiger's head), wreath, and scroll with motto. This kind of print may have been made as a cost-saving procedure for recording and storing dies, rather than setting up a press and pulling a proper proof.
Jim Joly Collection of Dameron-Pierson Co., Ltd. Steel Dies, Mss. 5071, Louisiana and Lower Mississippi Valley Collections, LSU Libraries.

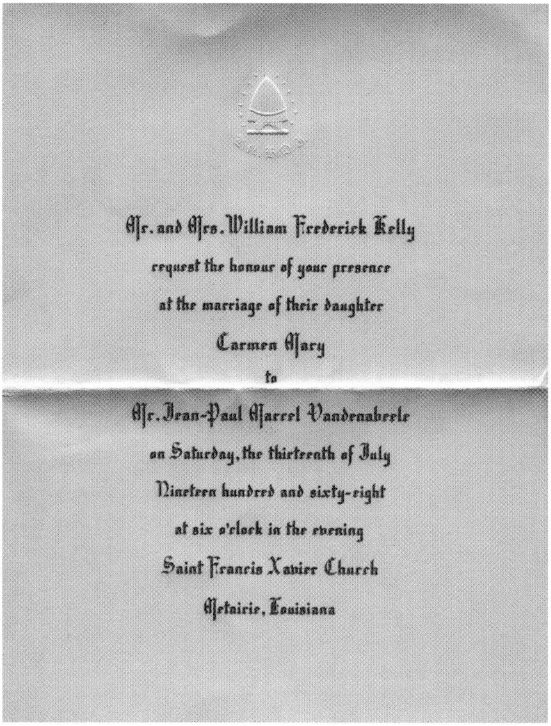

Mr. and Mrs. William Frederick Kelly
request the honour of your presence
at the marriage of their daughter
Carmen Mary
to
Mr. Jean-Paul Marcel Vandenabeele
on Saturday, the thirteenth of July
Nineteen hundred and sixty-eight
at six o'clock in the evening
Saint Francis Xavier Church
Metairie, Louisiana

Fig. 18, left:
Wedding invitation using family emblem of a beehive, New Orleans, 1968.
This crest is the mark for women in the client's family. As she explains, "Loosely the meaning is [that] Kelly females [are like] busy bees, [we] make [the] best honey...or, Irish women pick the best men, do the best work, and raise the best kids, something like that."

Fig. 19, right:
Detail of beehive emblem, blind-embossed on original wedding invitation for this client.
Printer unknown, New Orleans, 1968.

IN·ME·MEA·SPES·OMNIS
EX LIBRIS
Post

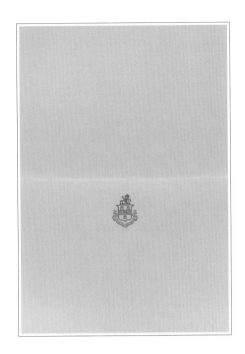

Fig. 20, top left: Bookplate for American philanthropist Marjorie Merriweather Post, 3 1/4 x 4 7/16 inches. An approximate translation of the motto on Ms. Post's coat of arms is "All My Hope Is in Myself."
Hillwood Estate, Museum & Gardens, Washington, DC; bequest of Marjorie Merriweather Post, 1973.

Fig. 21, top right: Personal folded note with engraved elements of Post's coat of arms: a crest (the lion), a shield, and scroll with motto, 5 1/8 x 7 6/16 inches (unfolded).
Hillwood Estate, Museum & Gardens, Washington, DC; bequest of Marjorie Merriweather Post, 1973.

Fig. 22, bottom: Gold-engraved coat of arms, Marjorie Merriwether Post, 4 x 6 inches.
Hillwood Estate, Museum & Gardens, Washington, DC; bequest of Marjorie Merriweather Post, 1973.

LOYAL EN TOUT
THROUGH
ICH DIEN
TENAX ET FIDUS

Fig. 23:
Various pieces of heraldic devices used as individual motifs or emblems; ciphers are also shown. *Lincoln Crest and Monogram Album* (London: Lincoln, 1860).
Collection of Joel Mason.
Photo by Eli Neugeboren.

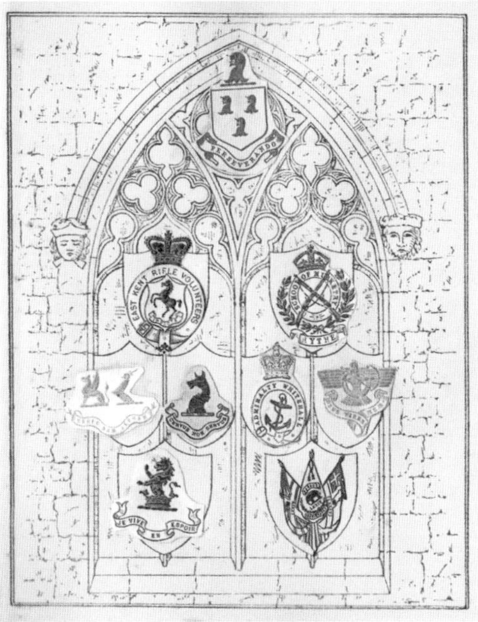
PERSEVERANDO
EAST KENT RIFLE VOLUNTEERS
HYTHE
ADMIRALTY WHITEHALL
JE VIVE EN ESPOIR

Fig. 24, top:
Engraved coat of arms, crests with motto and emblem. *Lincoln Crest and Monogram Album.*
Collection of Joel Mason.
Photo by Eli Neugeboren.

WOODBERRY FOREST
SMITH COLLEGE A.D. 1871

Fig. 25, bottom:
Single page showing engraved coat of arms, seals, and emblems. *Lincoln Crest and Monogram Album.*
Collection of Joel Mason.
Photo by Eli Neugeboren.

THE
TRANSPORTATION CLUB
NEW YORK
MASSACHUSETTS
INSTITUTE OF TECHNOLOGY.
1861
MENS ET MANUS
YALE UNIVERSITY
NEW HAVEN, CONN.
DAUGHTERS OF THE REVOLUTION
LIBERTY
HOME
AND
COUNTRY
GENERAL SOCIETY
1776
1891
FOR VALOUR

Fig. 26, above:
Single page showing various seals and emblems, engraved and embossed. *Lincoln Seal and Monogram Album.*

Collection of Joel Mason. Photo by Eli Neugeboren.

Fig. 27, opposite:
Engraved crests with motto. *Lincoln Seal and Monogram Album.*

Collection of Joel Mason. Photo by Eli Neugeboren.

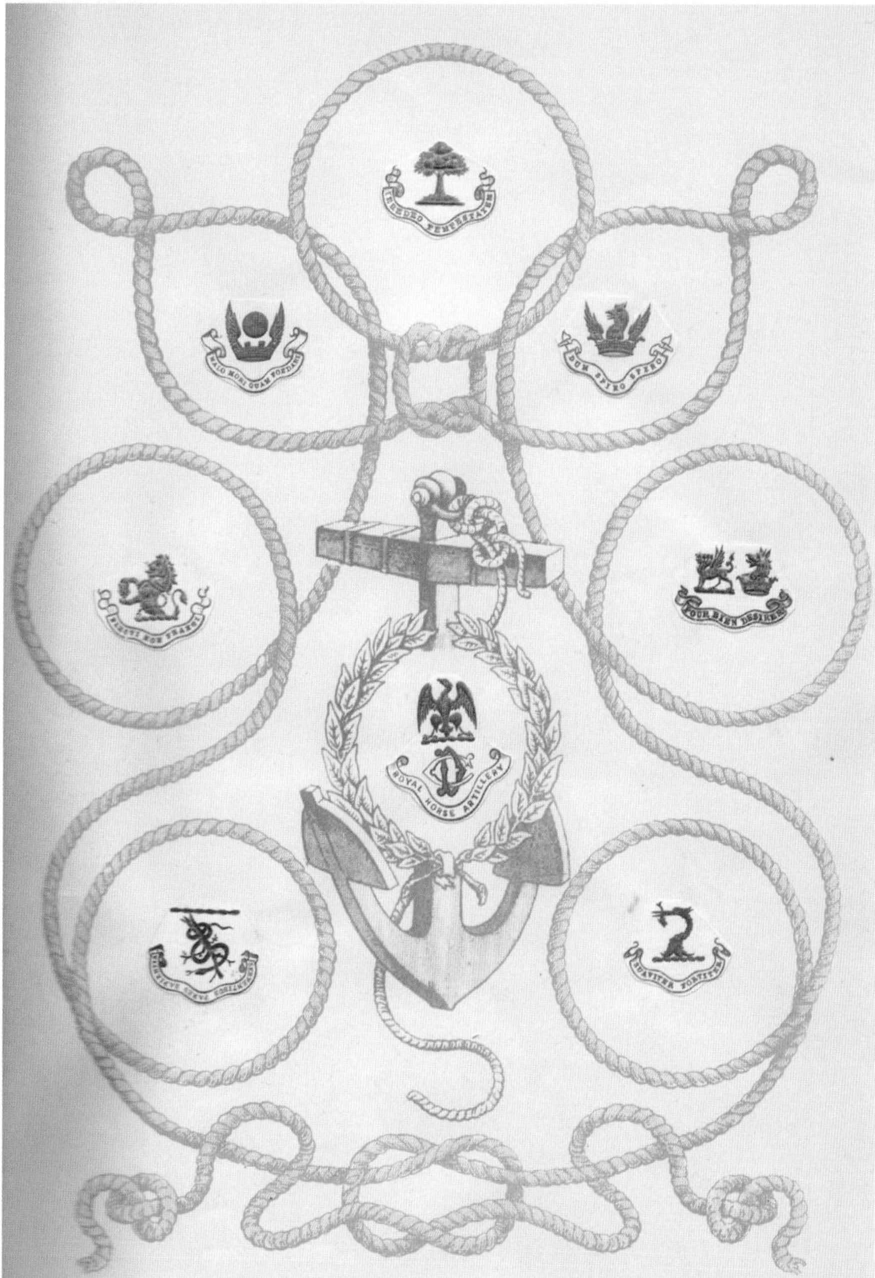
DUM SPIRO SPERO
ROYAL HORSE ARTILLERY
POUR BIEN DESIRER
SUAVITER FORTITER

Chapter Six

A HOW-TO OF ENGRAVING

For the purposes of this book, I have organized the production of engraved stationery into six stages: I. Researching visuals, II. Determining how the engraving is to be made, III. Preparing the artwork, IV. Engraving the plate or die, V. Selecting paper, VI. Printing.

I. RESEARCHING VISUALS

The first step is to narrow down what you want to engrave. The idea for the artwork might come from your imagination or from historic, contemporary, or cultural references. Over the years, I have amassed an archive of original samples, in addition to those people have given or sent to me. (Most of the visuals in this book come from my own collection.) You can build an archive of resource materials by collecting ephemera such as monograms, ciphers, and wrapping papers. [**Figs. 1, 2**] Decorative arts such as gun and knife engraving and textile, fine porcelain, china, silver, and pewter design are also good sources of inspiration, techniques, and support.[1] [**Fig. 3**]

Many historic engravings date from the era of the Industrial Revolution, when consumer goods were first produced in mass quantities. However, dynamic art need not be Victorian or old-fashioned in nature. I look to typography resources from the early twentieth century to the present for ideas and also find inspiration in the Aesthetic movement, the Vienna Secession, German Expressionism, the American Arts and Crafts movement, Dada, and Fluxus. [**Fig. 4**] I have discovered fantastic sources researching on the Internet and truly bizarre ephemera on the street. But whether you're using an old or a new reference, the artwork has to be translated into a suitable format for the engraving. [**Figs. 5–9**]

Fig. 1:
Specimen and idea sheet of vintage styles and an engraver's sketch based on an old design.
Created for client commission, New York, 2002.

Fig. 2:
Two-color hand-engraved cipher, an homage to one of the styles in the previous figure and the bottom figure on page 119.
Created for client commission, New York, 2002.

FM
R

Fig. 3, top:
Stationery photoengraved from a black-and-white photograph of eighteenth-century lace.
Created for Jeffery R. McKay, New York, 2006.

Fig. 4, bottom:
Hand-engraved metallic ink cipher (with bump to burnish the ink), inspired by a 1920 engraving by Alexander Koch, a German Aesthetic Movement calligrapher.
Created for client commission, Covington, Louisiana, 2008.

Fig. 5, top left:
The contemporary engraver's process, from ephemera to artwork (this image and the three following): grayscale conversion of a Victorian-era wrapping paper violet bouquet design silhouetted in Adobe Photoshop.
Created for client commission, New York, 2003.

Fig. 6, above:
Three violet stems were isolated and the ribbon retouched in Photoshop to wrap around the stems.

Fig. 7, top right:
Press proof of the three violets hand-engraved.

Karen LeDonne

Fig. 8, bottom:
Stationery engraved with the violets. The note sheets and envelopes were handmade. The envelope is fully lined, with bordering done by hand.
Created for client commission, New York, 2003.

II. DETERMINING HOW THE ENGRAVING IS TO BE MADE

Once you know what you want your design to look like, you need to determine how the engraving is to be made. This is important because each method may be compatible with a different kind of design or artwork. There are various approaches:

- Engrave it yourself.[2]
- Have it hand-engraved by someone using conventional methods (with a graver or burin). It's a wonderful idea to befriend an engraver and a great way to experience the process.
- Engrave it or have it engraved by someone with a pneumatic engraving system (discussed at more length below).
- Have it photoengraved by a commercial press.[3]

III. PREPARING THE ARTWORK

While some artistically gifted engravers can work directly from a photograph, most artwork for engraving begins with a sketch, so drawing proficiency is very important. The skills that distinguish great engraving from run-of-the-mill specimens are creativity and fine draftsmanship. In the late fifteenth and early sixteenth centuries, Dürer possessed not only a unique creative vision, but also the talent to draw what he saw in his mind. Today, with software proficiency, almost anyone can create a lovely engraving (albeit the photoengraved, or etched, kind), but truly remarkable hand engraving can only be accomplished by someone with imagination, good drawing skills, and the patience acquired by making painstaking cuts with engraving tools for many years.

PREPARING ART

HERE ARE THE FIVE STEPS TO FOLLOW WHEN PREPARING ARTWORK FOR AN ENGRAVER:[4]

1. DRAW A SKETCH OF WHAT YOU WANT ENGRAVED. THE BEST WAY TO DO THIS IS WITH PENCIL ON TRACING PAPER. [**Fig. 9**] I USE ARCHITECT'S CANARY PAPER THAT COMES IN ROLLS, AND A PENCIL WITH AN H HARDNESS GRADE.
2. DETERMINE IF THE ENGRAVER CAN WORK WITH A FINISHED PENCIL DRAWING OR IF YOU NEED TO SUPPLY LINE ART (ALL BLACK AND WHITE) TO ACHIEVE THE BEST RESULTS. SOME HAND-ENGRAVERS CAN WORK FROM A REALLY GOOD SKETCH, BUT IT'S BEST TO DISCUSS THIS WITH THE PERSON DOING THE ENGRAVING. [**Figs. 10–13**]
3. IF YOU ARE SUPPLYING LINE ART, FIND OUT IN WHAT FORM IT SHOULD BE SUPPLIED. MUCH OF PHOTOENGRAVING BEGINS WITH VECTOR-BASED ARTWORK CREATED USING GRAPHIC DESIGN SOFTWARE SUCH AS ADOBE'S ILLUSTRATOR OR FREEHAND OR CORELDRAW. [**Figs. 14–17**] START BY SCANNING YOUR SKETCH AND TRACE IT USING THE PEN TOOL, OR, IF YOU HAVE EXPERIENCE, DRAW DIRECTLY IN THE PROGRAM WITH BÉZIER CURVES. MAKE SURE THE STROKES AND FILLS ARE SPOT COLOR, 100 PERCENT BLACK. YOU CAN ALSO DRAW DIRECTLY INTO THE COMPUTER USING A WACOM TABLET WITH ITS DIGITAL PEN.
4. SCALE THE ART, PIXEL- OR VECTOR-BASED, TO FIT THE LAYOUT OF THE PIECE YOU ARE DESIGNING. INCLUDE MEASUREMENTS INDICATING HOW FAR THE ART APPEARS FROM THE

TOP, BOTTOM, AND LEFT AND RIGHT EDGES OF THE PAPER. BE VERY PRECISE. I PROVIDE MEASUREMENTS AS SMALL AS 1/64 OF AN INCH, ALTHOUGH ENGRAVING PRINTERS TEND TO WORK WITH LARGER INCREMENTS, SUCH AS 1/4 OR 1/8 OF AN INCH. ASK YOUR PRINTER FOR PREFERRED TOLERANCES.

5. PRINT OUT YOUR LAYOUT AND CHECK ALL MEASUREMENTS, THE FIDELITY OF THE ARTWORK, TYPOGRAPHY, SPELLING, AND PUNCTUATION (IF ANY).

Fig. 9:
Monogram and cipher sketches in graphite pencil on tracing paper.
Noel Martin, Covington, Louisiana, 1997.

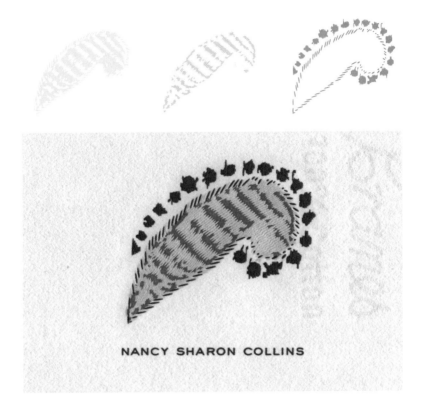

NANCY SHARON COLLINS

Fig. 10, opposite, top left: Original drawing for a monogram for a valentine, adjusted in Adobe Photoshop.
Created for Jeffery R. McKay, New York, 2004.

Fig. 11, opposite, top right: Hand-engraved monogram for valentine on Italian note card. The paper is hand bordered by Kartos of Montecatini, imported by San Lorenzo.
Created for Jeffery R. McKay, New York, 2004.

Fig. 12, opposite, middle: Digitized drawing of a cipher. Because this was faxed to a hand-engraver, the pixelation did not matter.
Created for client commission, New York, 2002.

Fig. 13, opposite, bottom: Hand-engraved cipher on onionskin calling card and fold-over note, and embroidered on 100 percent Italian linen napkin. The cipher is approximately five inches wide.
Created for client commission, New York, 2002.

Figs. 14–17, above: Details from a digital-to-engraved study: individual "stitches" were drawn in Adobe Illustrator to create a three-color, photoengraved replication of an embroidered paisley design. Actual size of paisley approximately ½ inch.
Commissioned by the author, New York, 2003.

IV. ENGRAVING THE PLATE OR DIE

The process of creating the engraving plate will vary depending on the approach you decide to take—photoengraving, pantograph engraving, pneumatic engraving, or hand engraving.

Photoengraving / Photoengraving is the most common form of commercial engraving. The process is as follows:

The pixel- or vector-based digital file is used to make a photographic piece of film, which records solid black and white and no midtones (no shades of gray). **[Figs. 18, 19]** The film is pressed against an intaglio plate that is prepared with a light-sensitive and acid-resistant coating. Usually this is done on a vacuum table so any air or space between the film and plate can be carefully managed when the artwork is transferred. There are two kinds of photosensitive intaglio plates, but for the most part positive photoresist plates with negative film are used for commercial engraving. Much as analog photography is developed in a darkroom, a positive photoresist plate is exposed to a controlled source of light, placed into a liquid developer, and then agitated in a bath to remove the coating on the plate where it was exposed to light through the clear parts of the film.

Exposure, developing, and a light washing renders the areas of the plate without coating acid-permeable. The plate is then placed into an acid bath, and the acid-permeable areas are etched into the metal plate, incising the art into the surface of the metal. Effectively, the acid performs the cut.

Special techniques in commercial photoengraving have been developed to simulate tone and value that look photographic. **[Fig. 20]** Large areas of solid color are more problematic in hand engraving and require special handling; otherwise the ink will gravitate to the margins. The leaves in figures 21 to 24, for example, were designed to take advantage of this effect. **[Figs. 21–24]**

Pantograph Engraving / My favorite engraving device, little known in the graphic design industry or anywhere else these days, is the Cronite Masterplate system.[5] While not many companies still offer it as a service, Cronite pantograph machines and Masterplates are still available. [**Figs. 25, 26**] This system is based on a vertical pantograph machine—a scaling transfer device—that manually allows the operator to trace a large image onto the surface of an engraving plate or die at a smaller scale. [**Fig. 27**] The Cronite system uses metal templates, or Masterplates, each about eighteen inches long and containing a complete alphabet, numerals, and some punctuation symbols. (They resemble the small green plastic templates used in drafting departments before the advent of computers.) Masterplates are available for more than three hundred lettering styles (see appendix A for examples of Masterplate styles). The operator traces each character from the template, a process that is facilitated by the large scale of the characters on the Masterplates, and the pantograph transfers it to the plate according to the degree of reduction set by the operator. Letterspacing issues, centering, leading, and general typographic considerations are all as good as the person operating the system, so results can vary. A skilled pantograph engraver's type is wholly unique, because, although it is created by a standardized system, each letter is composed, traced, and/or incised by hand. Some Masterplate styles have been digitized and developed into great and robust fonts (see appendix B for two examples). Many may look familiar because they are often used on wedding invitations, while others may appear quirky or of a certain vintage. [**Fig. 28**]

Pantographs are fairly simple, elegant devices, and they do not depend on electricity. To utilize the wonderful selection of styles, an enterprising designer would do well to locate, adopt, and learn to use one.

Pneumatic Engraving / A pneumatic engraving tool is like an elegant, miniature, air-powered jackhammer that drives the same exacting tools that hand-engravers use.[6] Developed in the mid-1960s and 1970s, they are used extensively to engrave firearms and collector's knives, glass,

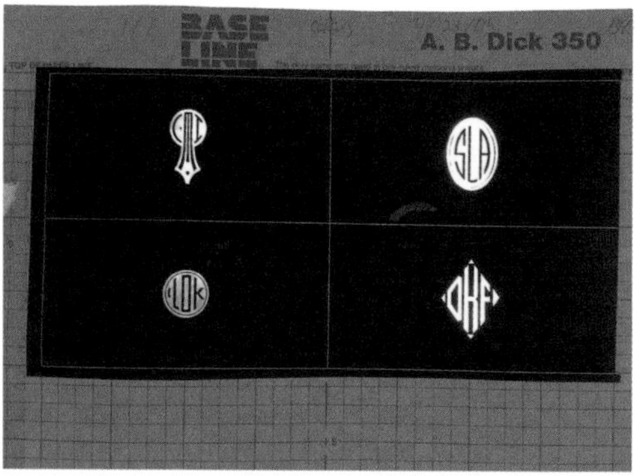
BASE LINE
A. B. Dick 350

Fig. 18, top left:
Film negative with cipher to be photoengraved on four note cards.
Beaver Creek Engraving, Dobson, North Carolina, 2009.

Fig. 19, bottom left:
Engraved cipher on Classic Crest fold-over notes from the above film negative.
Created for client commission, Covington, Louisiana, 2009.

Fig. 20, right:
Example of some of the varied effects possible with photoengraving. This page is one in a promotional booklet published for the seminal Designer Engraver Exchange meeting, designed by Steff Geissbuhler of Chermayeff & Geismar, New York.
Crane & Co., Dalton, Massachusetts, 1985.

Figs. 21–24, opposite:
Photoengraved leaves in yellow, red, green, and ochre on white onionskin.
Engraved for the author, New York, 1999.

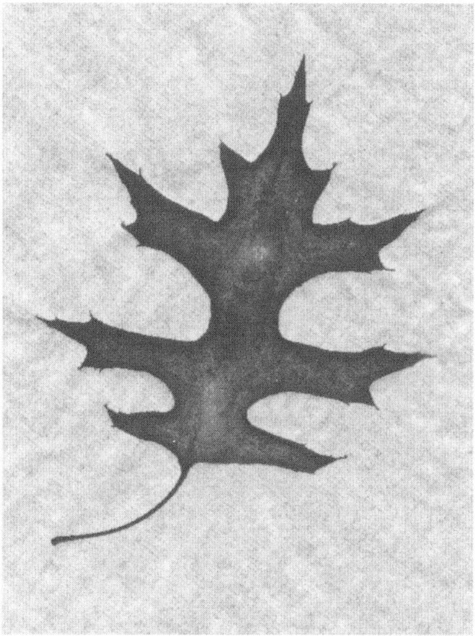

Cronite
COMPANY, INC.

ENGRAVING MACHINERY 79

The Universal Engraving Machine
Manufactured by The Cronite Co., Inc.

Fig. 25, top:
Cronite Masterplate.

Fig. 26, bottom left:
Detail of Cronite Masterplate lettering style catalog cover, hand-engraved on KromeKote cover stock.
Cronite Company, Inc., ca. 1970s.

Fig. 27, bottom right:
Illustration of Cronite's Universal Engraving Machine, a pantograph machine.
Robert N. Steffens, *Engraved Stationery Handbook* (New York: Cronite Company, 1950).

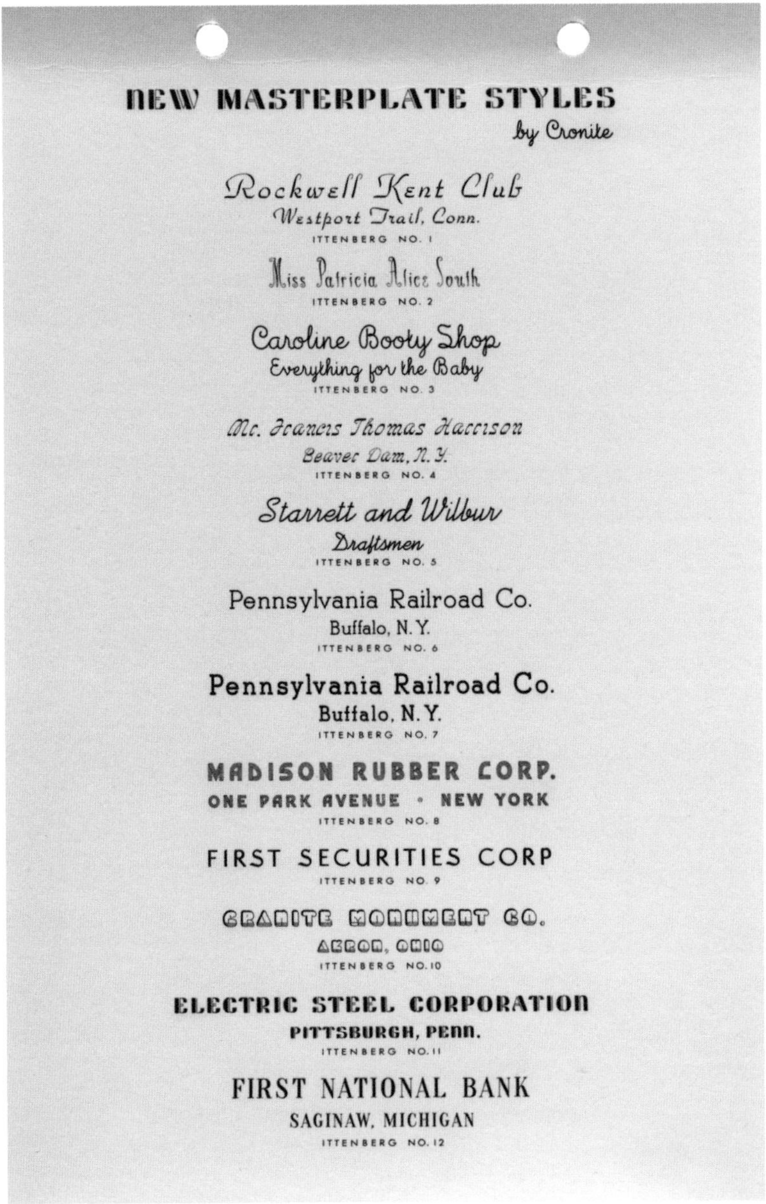

NEW MASTERPLATE STYLES
by Cronite

Rockwell Kent Club
Westport Trail, Conn.
ITTENBERG NO. 1

Miss Patricia Alice South
ITTENBERG NO. 2

Caroline Booty Shop
Everything for the Baby
ITTENBERG NO. 3

Mr. Francis Thomas Harrison
Beaver Dam, N. Y.
ITTENBERG NO. 4

Starrett and Wilbur
Draftsmen
ITTENBERG NO. 5

Pennsylvania Railroad Co.
Buffalo, N. Y.
ITTENBERG NO. 6

Pennsylvania Railroad Co.
Buffalo, N. Y.
ITTENBERG NO. 7

MADISON RUBBER CORP.
ONE PARK AVENUE • NEW YORK
ITTENBERG NO. 8

FIRST SECURITIES CORP
ITTENBERG NO. 9

GRANITE MONUMENT CO.
AKRON, OHIO
ITTENBERG NO. 10

ELECTRIC STEEL CORPORATION
PITTSBURGH, PENN.
ITTENBERG NO. 11

FIRST NATIONAL BANK
SAGINAW, MICHIGAN
ITTENBERG NO. 12

Fig. 28:
Page from the Masterplate catalog.

and fine stonework, and to engrave plates and dies for social stationery and prints. The tool is a great investment for newly minted engravers, because one can learn to use it in a fraction of the time it takes to master engraving solely with a graver or burin.

Hand Engraving / The art of hand engraving means mastering the relationship between the tool and the surface on which a design is engraved. Koichi Yamamoto, an assistant professor of printmaking at the University of Tennessee, Knoxville, School of Art, explains it this way:

> When I was learning copper engraving in Bratislava, Slovakia, my professor Dusan Kallay told me, "First you have to learn ice skating." I never excelled at that, but became proficient at snowboarding while living in Utah. It's the process of understanding the material you are carving, whether ice, snow, wood, or copper.[7]

One of the most crucial and daunting steps in the engraving process is transferring artwork to the surface upon which the engraving is performed. Most commercial engraving plates are 16 gauge, or 0.06 inches, in thickness. Copperplates are traditional, although steel, zinc, and magnesium are also used. Dies are thicker, usually made out of steel, and vary in depth, but half an inch appears to be the norm. Whereas the original art for photoengraving looks much like the end result, in hand engraving, the difference between the original artwork and the actual cut can be quite marked. This is because the artwork itself serves as a general idea for what the engraver eventually creates (drawing with pencil, pixels, or Bézier curves is very different from cutting into metal). Not only is each cut completely unique, the way each engraver interprets a design is also specific to that artisan's creativity and ability. Artwork may be drawn directly on a plate or die, traced from an original source with a graphite pencil, or applied with the use of a pantograph.[8] **[Fig. 29]** Chinese white, special waxes, and gelatins are sometimes used to make the surface of the metal more receptive to a drawing.

The sharpness of the engraving tool is crucial for cutting the design, and engravers take great care of their tools. Straight lines are cut freehand or with a ruling machine; all lines going in the same direction are cut with the plate fixed in the same place. Cross-hatching is achieved by making a series of parallel lines, then turning the plate and going over the same area with a new series of parallel lines at a different angle. Curved designs and calligraphic engraving are achieved in a similar fashion: the engraver cuts all of the lines at one angle before turning the plate and cutting at the next angle. An accomplished engraver will cut a tight curve by holding the graver in one place and gradually turning the plate beneath it.

A sharp graver literally pushes metal out of the way, producing a burr, a curl of the cut material. At the end of a cut, a master engraver will be able to lift the burr completely out, making a pleasing terminal or a long, gracefully tapering tail. If part or all of the burr is left, a square or lozenge graver may be used to cut it off and finish the edges. The resulting spurs are the telltale indication of an engraving: no other printmaking process leaves these distinctive marks. In the final stage of engraving, any points where lines adjoin are finessed to make them uniform and clean. [**Figs. 30–33**]

Mistakes can be mended by pushing the surface back up by punching the plate from the reverse, and then burnishing it back to the same

Fig. 29:
Original graphite pencil drawing of a cipher on tracing paper with graphite on the back.
Noel Martin, Covington, Louisiana, 1999.

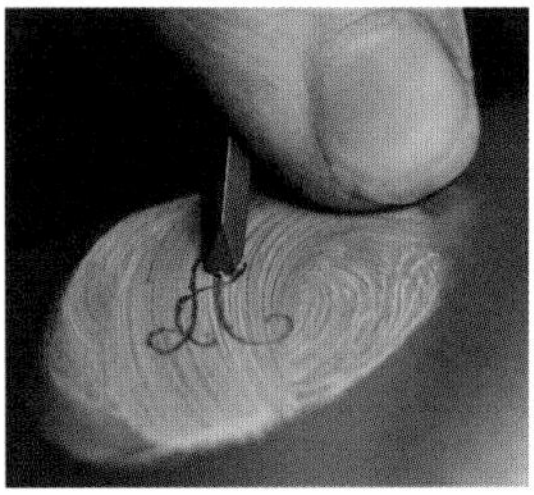
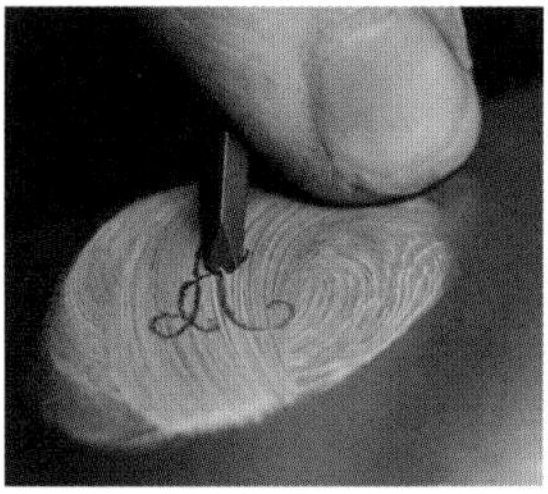
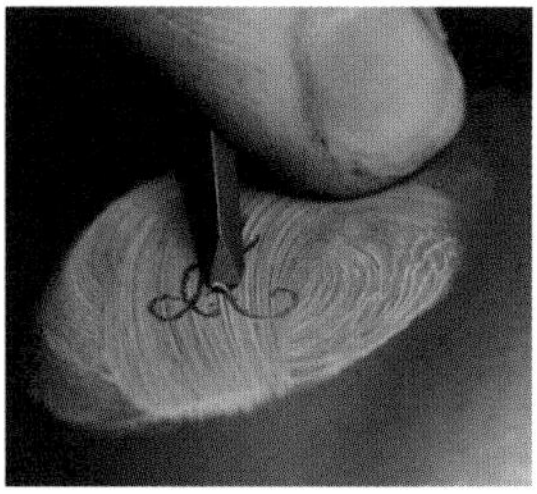

Figs. 30 – 32, top row:
Uppercase script *A* drawn in graphite pencil on Chinese white smudged with a finger on a steel plate for engraving.
Ed DeLorge, Houma, Louisiana, 2011.

—

The graver produces a burr, which can be seen at the forwardmost tip of the engraving tool.

—

As the graver is pushed forward, the burr increases in length and begins to curl.

Fig. 33, middle:
The finished engraved letter.

Fig. 34, bottom:
The backside of a ½-inch-thick steel engraving die with four drilled holes for punching up mistakes on the surface of the front of the die.

level as the rest of the surface. [**Fig. 34**] Though never ideal, this type of mending on large, elaborate engravings is preferable to starting all over again on a new plate.[9]

V. SELECTING PAPER

Some engraving companies will handle everything in-house—making the plate, running the press, buying the paper and envelopes, and even helping with technical issues in the preparation of your artwork—but you will probably pay a premium for these services. In other cases, and depending upon your design, you may need to have your plate or die cut by one craftsman and printed by another, as not all engravers handle their own printing. Some firms that engrave and print may not be able to suggest interesting papers, envelopes, or card stock. In this case, discuss your thoughts about paper with both the printer and the engraver, making sure the process is best served by your choice.

If you provide your own stock, you may need to supply 10 to 20 percent more paper than the printer will yield to allow for overs, paper or envelopes spoiled during the makeready; printing; and binding, finishing, and packing processes. Engraving can be printed on almost any kind of paper, from very thin sheets to very thick card stock or even cardboard. [**Figs. 35–37**] The paper you choose needs to be of uniform size for an engraver to feed through the printing process, so you may want to find papers ready for printing at a local stationery store that sells paper stock and envelopes in bulk. Alternatively, there are now many online paper retailers. However, if you order paper over the Internet, make sure to get some samples first so you can see the paper's actual color and feel its texture and weight. Sometimes it is possible to find interesting leftover paper stock in unexpected places: check companies going out of business, garage or tag sales, and secondhand stores. [**Fig. 38**] In 1999 I rediscovered onionskin, one of the oldest types of paper used for long-distance correspondence, at a printer that was getting rid of leftover stock. Although

NANCY SHARON COLLINS
NANCY SHARON COLLINS, STATIONER
ENGRAVING
HAND ENGRAVED SOCIAL STATIONERY
GRAPHIC DESIGN
EDUCATION
NANCY SHARON COLLINS, STATIONER
73 SPRING STREET # 505
NEW YORK CITY 10012
FAX 431 5610
NANCY SHARON COLLINS
73 SPRING STREET #505
NEW YORK CITY 10012
FAX 431 5610

Fig. 35, above:
Several examples showing a wide variety of papers, and weights of paper, upon which the same lettering style has been engraved.

Artscroll Printing, New York, and Hart Engraving, Milwaukee, commissioned by the author, 1997 to 2008.

Fig. 36, opposite, top:
Line Block lettering style engraved on ultra-thin, vintage #9, cockle finish, 25 percent cotton onionskin paper and four-ply, 100 percent cotton museum board (1⁄16-inch thick).

Commissioned by the author, New York, 1997 and 2008.

Fig. 37, opposite, bottom:
Vintage 9# Tuscon (orange) manifold paper and black, four-ply museum board Legion Paper. One piece of this museum board is as thick as a stack of approximately thirty-four sheets of onionskin or manifold copy paper. Manifold, a type of onion-skin paper, was once used in offices for making duplicate copies with carbon paper—the different colors served as a color coding system for filing correspondence.

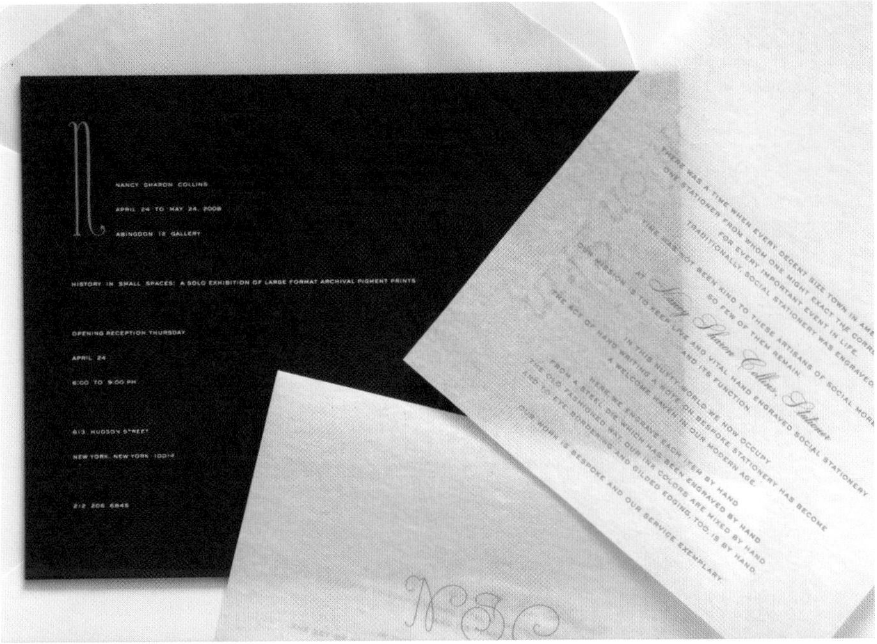
NANCY SHARON COLLINS
APRIL 24 TO MAY 24, 2008
ABINGDON 12 GALLERY
HISTORY IN SMALL SPACES: A SOLO EXHIBITION OF LARGE FORMAT ARCHIVAL PIGMENT PRINTS
OPENING RECEPTION THURSDAY
APRIL 24
6:00 TO 9:00 PM
613 HUDSON STREET
NEW YORK, NEW YORK 10014
212 206 6845
FOR EVERY IMPORTANT EVENT IN LIFE.
SO FEW OF THEM REMAIN.
AT Nancy Sharon Collins, Stationer
OUR MISSION IS TO KEEP LIVE AND VITAL HAND ENGRAVED SOCIAL STATIONERY
AND ITS FUNCTION.
IN THIS NUTTY WORLD WE NOW OCCUPY
THE ACT OF HAND WRITING A NOTE ON BESPOKE STATIONERY HAS BECOME
A WELCOME HAVEN IN OUR MODERN AGE.
HERE WE ENGRAVE EACH ITEM BY HAND
FROM A STEEL DIE WHICH HAS BEEN ENGRAVED BY HAND
THE OLD FASHIONED WAY, OUR INK COLORS ARE MIXED BY HAND
AND TO EYE, BORDERING AND GILDED EDGING, TOO, IS BY HAND.
OUR WORK IS BESPOKE AND OUR SERVICE EXEMPLARY.

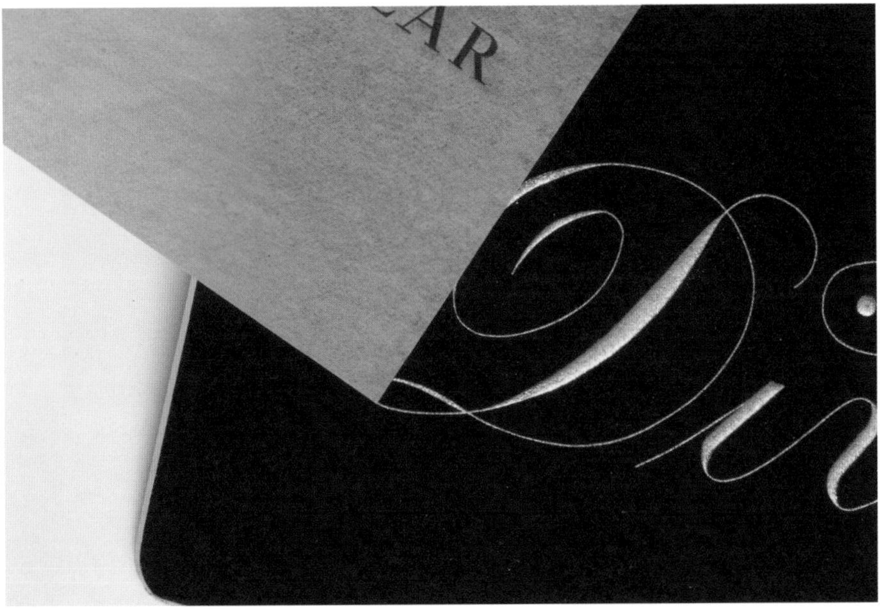

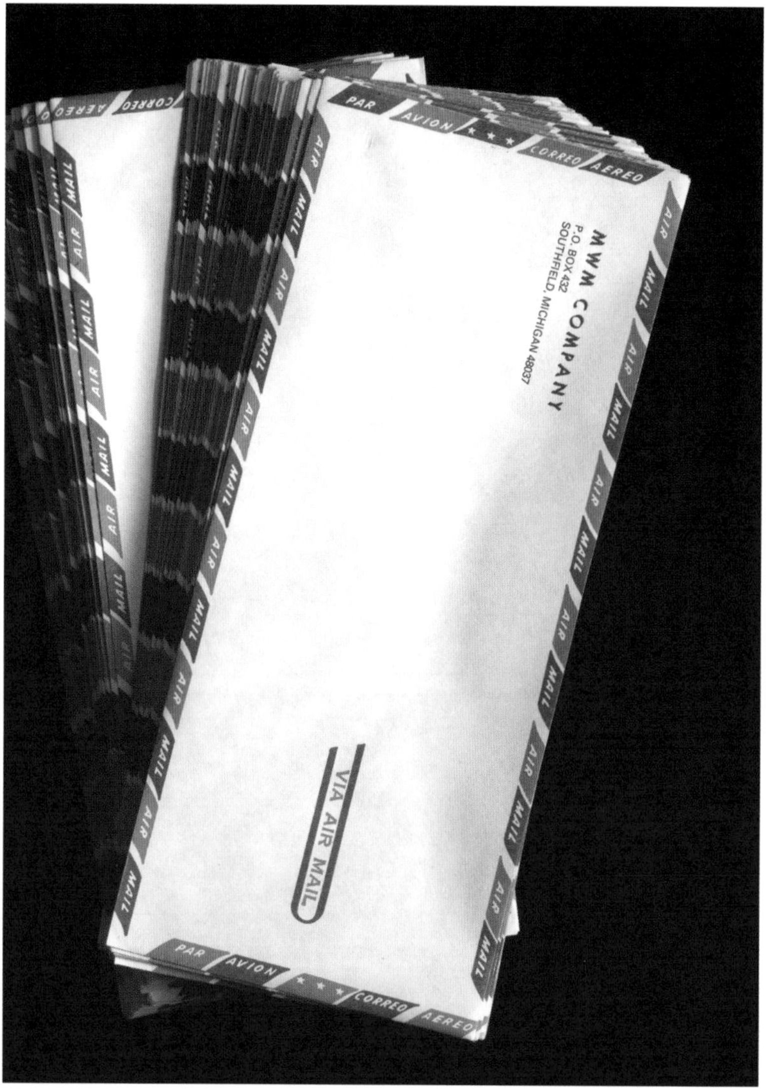
PAR AVION
CORREO AEREO
AIR MAIL
MWM COMPANY
P.O. BOX 432
SOUTHFIELD, MICHIGAN 48037
VIA AIR MAIL

Fig. 38:
Airmail envelopes from the Midwest Waste Material Company, Detroit, Michigan, for whom the author's father worked.

Fig. 39:
Various colors and finishes of vintage 9# onionskin and manifold paper.

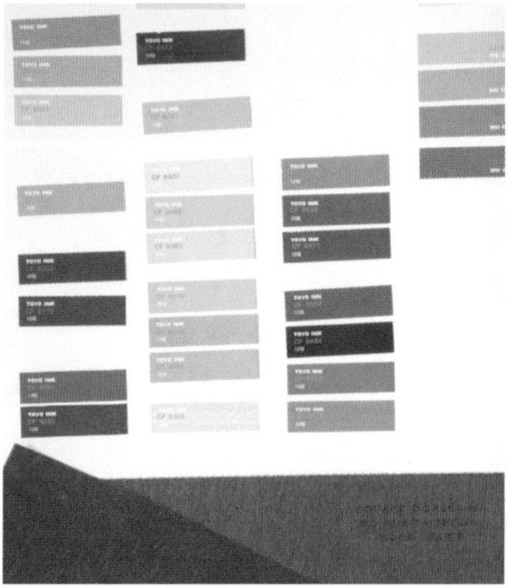

Fig. 40:
Hand-engraved cipher in turquoise water-based ink on silk-screened onionskin paper, developed from a color study for the launch of a fragrance. The ink is varnish-based, so it appears shiny, like varnish-finished furniture.
Commissioned by the author, New York, 2003.

Fig. 41:
Toyo Color Finder spot color chips, part of the study.
Commissioned by the author, New York, 2001.

onionskin was once manufactured in a rainbow of colors, today it is tough to find it in anything other than white. It is made with a smooth finish and a puckered one, called "cockle." [**Fig. 39**] Onionskin typically has some cotton content, making it durable and strong. Fountain pen, felt tip, and calligraphy inks make beautiful marks on its surface, and it is an excellent receiver of color and pigment, perhaps because of its high rag content. For the launch of a client's new fragrance, I once commissioned a chromatic study silk-screened on onionskin. This was when printers were converting from high-VOC (volatile organic compound) inks, and some, like my silk screener, were still willing to use varnish-based inks. [**Figs. 40, 41**]

VI. PRINTING

Primarily, there are two types of presses used for engraving: traditional intaglio presses and die stamping presses, which are used with commercially engraved plates and dies.[10] Intaglio printing is done with a rolling press, which consists of a horizontal bed that passes between two large, heavy metal cylinders called drums. In this process an intaglio plate is inked, wiped by hand, and placed on the bed. Wetted paper is positioned on top of the plate, and large felt blankets (usually wool) of different thicknesses are set on top of the paper. When the bed is rolled between the drums, the blankets help to evenly distribute pressure across the paper and push it into the inked grooves of the plate for the ink transfer. A good way to experience this historic process is to take an intaglio printmaking class at your local college or university. Artists continue to use intaglio printing as a creative means of expression, either by collaborating with a printmaker or working as a modern-day *peinter-graveur*. [**Fig. 42**]

There are four steps to produce engraved stationery on a commercial die stamping press: prepress; makeready; the press run (or "on press"); and the binding, finishing, packing, and delivery processes.

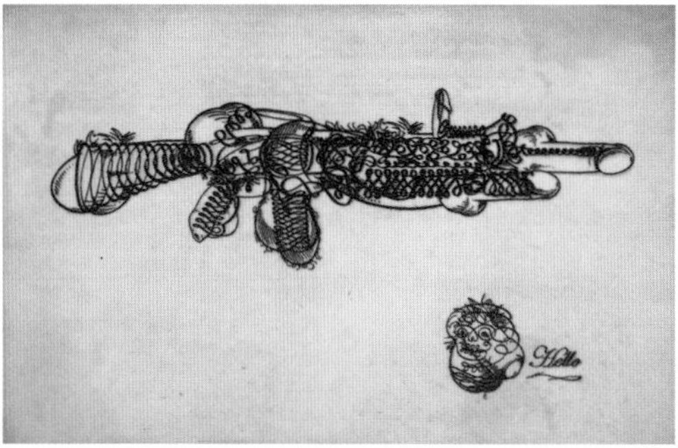
Hello

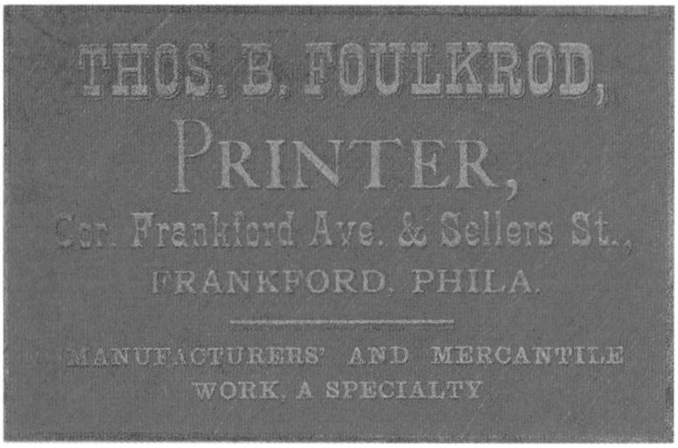
THOS. B. FOULKROD,
PRINTER,
Cor. Frankford Ave. & Sellers St.,
FRANKFORD, PHILA.
MANUFACTURERS' AND MERCANTILE
WORK, A SPECIALTY

Fig. 42, top:
Say Hello, collaborative etching by Tim Dooley and Aaron Wilson, honoring the legacy of print engraving, calligraphy, and social commentary.
Midwest Pressed, Cedar Falls, Iowa, 2007.

Fig. 43, middle:
Press proofs of hand-engraved cipher plate on three different paper stocks with a very light gray ink.
Emily DeLorge, Houma, Louisiana, 2011.

Fig. 44, bottom:
Trade card in gold metallic ink.
Collection of Richard D. Sheaff.

Prepress / Artwork for commercial engraving is now generated in the form of a digital file with artwork at exact scale and placement. As part of the prepress process, the designer or client specifies color, usually from the Pantone Matching System (PMS), though in some cases ink is mixed by hand on press. Usually, each ink color on a die stamping press goes down one at a time, requiring an individual plate and makeready for that color alone. (The ink used in commercial engraving is vegetablebased and watersoluble.[11]) Before approving a job for production, you should insist on a press proof. Press runs for social stationery are relatively small, so making adjustments to ink color can be accommodated while you stand there. If your color is difficult to get right, you should expect to pay extra for the press person's additional time. Corporate projects require more planning because they generally have larger print runs. Some designs require the coordination of several elements to match chromatically.[12] [**Fig. 43**] Knowing a bit about the different qualities of ink and paper is helpful when specifying engraving jobs, as some inks are very dense and opaque (e.g., black and reds), while others are less so (e.g., some blues may have unexpected qualities, and yellows can appear thin). Metallic inks present their own challenges for both printmaker and press person, so it is best to consult with your engravers before choosing metallic ink.[13] [**Fig. 44**]

Makeready / The makeready is all the steps required to prepare a press for printing. While methods vary from shop to shop, in general a plate or die is affixed to the press opposite a paperboard (or polymer) counter, which helps direct the extreme pressure and ink from the plate or die onto the paper. Essentially the plate is the female component and the counter is the male. Each counter is cut, by hand or using a mold, to replicate the design in relief. An overlay is placed over the counter, which softens the effect of the bruise. Guides are set for the exact positioning of each piece of stationery, envelope, or card. This is especially important with multicolor jobs where registration is crucial. Once the makeready is complete, the press run begins.

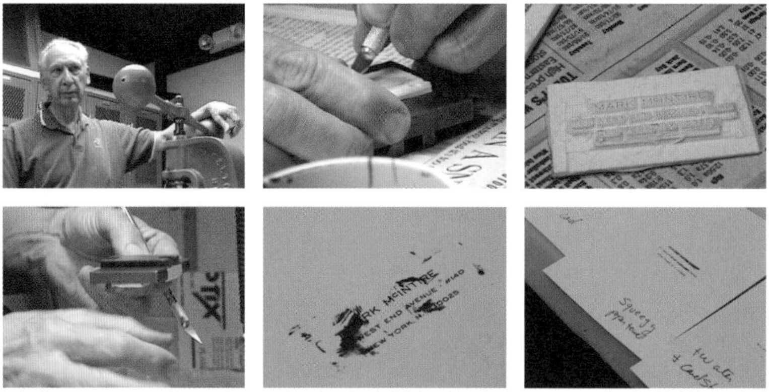

Seasons Greetings

Fig. 45, top:
Still captures from video of a vintage engraving proofing press demonstration at Loyola University, New Orleans, 2010. Contemporary water-based ink was used in this demo on a one-hundred-year-old machine that was engineered for varnish-based ink, which dries much more slowly than water-based ink. The ink dried before a proper impression could be created.

Fig. 46, bottom left:
Force on the proofing press at Loyola. The amount of pressure with which the ram forces a plate or die against the piece of paper is generally two tons per square inch.

Fig. 47, bottom right:
Seasons Greetings cards on four-ply, 100 percent cotton museum board, hand gilded and with radiused corners.
Commissioned by the author, New York, 2002.

Press run / Each card or piece of paper is positioned so it is in between the plate or die and the counter. Extreme pressure is applied, by way of a force or ram, with the counter helping to precisely transfer the ink. Once the plate is released, the paper retains the ink, the raised quality, and the distinctive bruise. [**Figs. 45, 46**]

While some presses still require each piece of paper, envelope, or card to be fed manually, one at a time, many automatic functions, such as paper feeding, inking, and plate wiping, are now available on commercial presses.[14]

Before the use of water-based inks, which dry quickly, the drying time for commercially engraved stationery was measured in multiples of days (depending on ambient temperature and humidity). Therefore, a piece of tissue paper was placed in between each completed print to prevent the ink offsetting onto the back of the print stacked on top of it. Though no longer serving a functional purpose, the delicate tissue sheet is still used as a formal lagniappe in some wedding invitation suites.[15]

Bindery, finishing, packing, and delivery / Engraved stationery pieces are particularly conducive to embellishment, such as decorative borders, colors, or gilded edges. [**Fig. 47**] Though bordering and gilding can be done prepress, these additional niceties are generally considered bindery and finishing work and may be performed by either the printer or a specialty vendor. Other binding and finishing operations include special folding and assembly, envelope lining, and various book bindings.

One of the most important and least considered stages in an engraving job is packing and delivery. With the considerable amount of time, resources, and energy that go into engraved stationery, making sure that each piece is packed so it does not rub, offset, or get damaged is crucial. An entire print run can be ruined by thoughtless handling and packing. Paper is heavy, but corners are very susceptible to dents, and even a small blemish on a hand-engraved card renders it unacceptable.

THE ART OF ENGRAVING

MARJORIE B. COHN

Art connoisseurs and scholars usually think about engraving chronologically, noting how the spare engraved outlines of the mid-fifteenth century, shaded with minimal hatchings, blossom over the next four hundred years into nets of stippled tone, calligraphic swirls, and florid expansions of geometric tracery, often combined in the same image—as they are on one of the few remnants of engraving still commonplace, our currency. Historians of engraving have chosen various points to break off their studies. Some have been fascinated by the divisive issue of origin; was engraving invented in the Upper Rhine, the southwestern region of modern Germany, along with book printing, or was it invented in Italy, as an adaptation of shop practice by gold- and silversmiths? Others follow the tale of engraving to its creative climax in the first quarter of the sixteenth century, when the three men still considered its most brilliant practitioners, the German Albrecht Dürer, the Dutchman Lucas van Leyden, and the Italian Marcantonio Raimondi, flourished.

Marcantonio's engraved art was not only a culmination; it began what some chroniclers conceive as the corrupting worm—reproduction. Yet he was rewarded in his own lifetime and is still celebrated today. The difficulty with traditional engraving is this: it is both a technical challenge, requiring the ability to carve metal with precision and delicacy, and an aesthetic one, demanding skill as a draftsman and a designer. These multiple aptitudes are rarely found in the same person; even more exceptional is the accomplished engraver who is also an imaginative genius. Reproductive engraving allowed the less-than-complete printmaker to combine technical facility with the products of another person, one with artistic training and talent, translating into black lines on white paper the tones, colors, and shapes created by a painter or a sculptor. Marcantonio allied himself with the painter Raphael, and the two Italians are considered founders of the specialization that kept engraving progressive and profitable through the next three centuries, until the invention of the photograph doomed handmade reproductions.

Still other historians of engraving end their consideration of the technique and its achievements at the point when etching entered the picture, in full flood by the beginning of the seventeenth century. Like engraving, etching is an intaglio printing technique; grooves in the surface of a matrix, which in both cases is a metal plate, hold ink that is released onto paper through the action of a press, usually a set of rollers like an old-fashioned laundry wringer. In etching, however, the grooves are created through chemical action rather than carving, allowing artists to sketch their original designs with a freedom unobtainable by the muscular discipline enforced by engraving. Since both techniques utilize the same surface, fast and easy etching was quickly incorporated into the engraver's repertoire, especially as a device to "forward" the plate, that is, to rapidly corrode into the plate the basics of an entire design, leaving tedious, delicate finishing touches to the engraver's burin.

Not all connoisseurs of engraving have thought of etching as the easy way out. While some schools, especially the French, remained resolutely pure, others, such as the British, accepted and even valued etching's characteristically rugose line, especially in the depiction of landscape elements—tree bark, rocks—where it played off attractively against the clean engraved traces of clouds or the flesh and drapery of whatever nymphs, saints, or peasants populated the scene. Even after the invention of photography, for a while an engraving, perhaps in combination with etching, was considered more purified, more authentic, as a reproduction of a masterwork than the blurry tones, filled with incident and accident, of the photographic print.

What is lacking from almost all historical studies of engraving, however, is an appreciation of the huge variety of styles that engravers over the centuries have worked in. Consider the engraved reproduction by Louis Cossin of a painted portrait of Louis Roupert, a French seventeenth-century ornament printmaker and goldsmith. [**Fig. 1**] It is a unique statement about the disparity between the representation of

Fig. 1:
Louis Cossin (1627–1686),
Portrait of Louis Roupert, 1668,
after a painting by Pierre Rabon.
Engraving plate: 15.2 x 21.4 cm
(6 x 8 7/16 inches), Harvard Art Museums/
Fogg Museum, anonymous loan in
honor of Edith I. Welch, 24.1997.

a painted version of reality and that of a contrived decorative embellishment. Roupert is seen seated holding a page of his own design, an elaborate foliate pattern. On the table next to him lie the tools of his trade—burins, calipers, a double-ended chalk holder, a scribing point, a sharpening stone, pliers, metal shears, even a feather brush to dust away the curls of metal as he carves them from his creation. The object itself, the product of Roupert's craft, is missing; the portraitist has chosen instead to show his inspiration. On the table stands a vase, which, like the rest of the scene, is engraved with utmost delicate verisimilitude. It is a footed globe of glass, off which a reflection glistens and in which the stems of the foliage it contains are dimly shaded. Note that this vase is also a tool: water-filled glass spheres were used to magnify the light of a candle, to enable the engraver to work at night. But out of this vase springs a fantastic bouquet! Rather than using the standard seventeenth-century syntax for engraved reality—fine swelling and tapering parallel lines and measured crosshatching—Cossin (or perhaps Roupert himself?) has engraved an ornament appropriate to watch cases, snuff boxes, and other precious *objets de vertu*.

From this fabulous abstract foliage it is easy to enter the even more cerebral world of letters. The calligraphic engraver and the type cutter—a kind of engraver—develop every form from pure imagination (necessarily combined with legibility). All the techniques, disciplines, habits, and discoveries of more than five hundred years of engravings are fair game when engraving a flourish, monogram, or cipher on a piece of stationery. In this book twenty-first-century engravers can find inspiration in the immense variety of engraved social stationery that can serve so many different ends.

AFTERWORD

The story of American commercial engraving in the twenty-first century is similar to that of manufacturing industries all over the United States: continuing decline appears inevitable. While it is true and deeply saddening that the demise of older, small print and engraving shops continues at a precipitous rate, the trajectory of this downward trend is countered and balanced by an increase in young letter-writing enthusiasts and hardcore lettering arts practitioners.

At the end of 2010, the popular clothing retailer J. Crew announced a new line of stationery, a joint venture with an engraver. The growing popularity of letter-writing on proper stationery must have inspired the company's marketing department to start an engraved line for its brand. In January 2011, the Louisiana Engravers Society was inaugurated, bringing together a vital but disparate community of engravers and print engraving aficionados, including the author. The fact that there are enough engravers and aficionados in the area to form a society demonstrates that the culture of New Orleans appreciates history and fosters creativity. What is striking is that three of the society's members are under the age of thirty. Through its extended family of contacts, the group has access to practitioners, young and old, across the country.

In another recent development, online font distributors are launching a range of engraving lettering styles from the twentieth century. That contemporary font developers and marketers recognize the aesthetic and useful value of these beautiful, romantic, and nostalgic engraving styles signifies their viability in the modern digital world.

Also promising is the fact that several venerable and beloved engraved stationers that had shut their doors have come back to life. Mrs. John L. Strong, a legendary New York engraving company that catered to stars and the social register since 1929, has once again opened its signature Madison Avenue suite of offices. Pineider, the famed Italian paper merchant and stationer (the author's personal favorite) is once again distributed in Europe and the United States. And there are new stationery companies investing in engraving.

Will engraving ever return to its lofty status and profound historic greatness? Probably not. Will engraving remain a vital tool for image making, a dynamic art, and a lively craft? Most decidedly yes. As more of us access and use it in our design work, learn how to engrave, and make or buy engraved stationery, a new generation of customers will learn its function, beauty, and appeal. Perhaps, someday, engraving will go viral.

ACKNOWLEDGMENTS

First, my thanks to those who read my manuscript and gave invaluable comments: Nancy Bernardo; Alan Czaplicki; William Kitchens; Paul Dean; Mark Simonson; and Richard Sheaff, who also provided many images. Second, to Marjorie B. Cohn and Ellen Lupton for their essay and foreword, respectively. Third, to those who contributed vital elements and information for this book: Robert Steffens, Tommy Flax, Brian and Nancy Hart, Rick Doby, Noel Martin, Dave Perkins, Elliot Schwartz, Joe Fontana, Harris Griggs and the International Engraved Graphics Association board of directors. Fourth, to those whose research so helped this story: John Magill, Pamela Arceneaux, Amelia J. Hugill-Fontanel, Keith Finley, Elaine Smythe, Judy Bolton, Germain Bienvenu, Jonathan G. Harrell, Kristen Regina, Sam Wright, Joel Mason, Eli Neugeboren, Peter Harrington, Lawrence Benjamin Lewis, Carol Sue Furnish, Allan Haley, Steve Bonoff, Deanna Gentile, and Burkey Belser, as well as to David Shields, who made it possible for me to research for a week at the Harry Ransom Center, University of Texas at Austin. I would also like to thank: Steve Matteson, Bill Davis, Terrance Weinzierl, and Emily DeLorge for creating the digital fonts associated with this book; Martin Hutner, J. Fernando Peña, Mark Schreyer, James Ehlers, Lora Shore, Ed DeLorge, Jessica M. Kyler,

Lynn Swann, Sean King, and Marissa Winkler for specific images sourced for this book; Frank Martinez, Esq., for his crackerjack legal advice; Kyle Petrozza for help with photography and technical issues; and Yvette Rutledge, Vince Mitchell, Daniela Marx, and Lissi Erwin for their unflagging belief and support in all things letter arts related. Special thanks to: Jeffery McKay for letting me edit this book while being his guest and irritating him with all of my digital media; and my family, who has always believed in me, especially my late mother, Charlotte Kaufman Feldman, who taught me to see the world in an organized and highly aesthetic fashion, and my late husband, John Mack Collins, who shared that vision.

APPENDIX

A

MASTERPLATE STYLES

Engravers
Letter Styles
The CRONITE Co.
HUDSON BLVD. AT 88TH STREET
NORTH BERGEN, N.J.

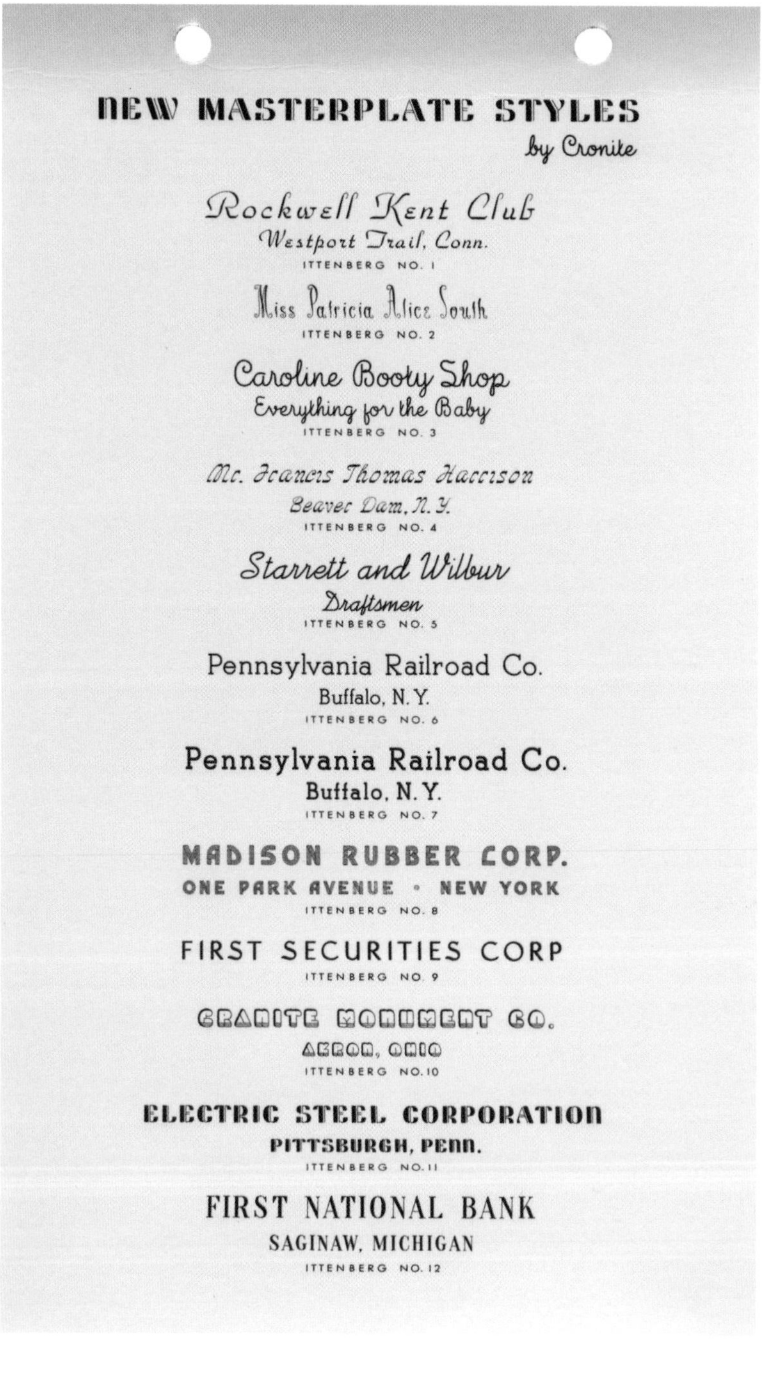

NEW MASTERPLATE STYLES
by Cronite

Rockwell Kent Club
Westport Trail, Conn.
ITTENBERG NO. 1

Miss Patricia Alice South
ITTENBERG NO. 2

Caroline Booty Shop
Everything for the Baby
ITTENBERG NO. 3

Mr. Francis Thomas Harrison
Beaver Dam, N. Y.
ITTENBERG NO. 4

Starrett and Wilbur
Draftsmen
ITTENBERG NO. 5

Pennsylvania Railroad Co.
Buffalo, N. Y.
ITTENBERG NO. 6

Pennsylvania Railroad Co.
Buffalo, N. Y.
ITTENBERG NO. 7

MADISON RUBBER CORP.
ONE PARK AVENUE • NEW YORK
ITTENBERG NO. 8

FIRST SECURITIES CORP
ITTENBERG NO. 9

GRANITE MONUMENT CO.
AKRON, OHIO
ITTENBERG NO. 10

ELECTRIC STEEL CORPORATION
PITTSBURGH, PENN.
ITTENBERG NO. 11

FIRST NATIONAL BANK
SAGINAW, MICHIGAN
ITTENBERG NO. 12

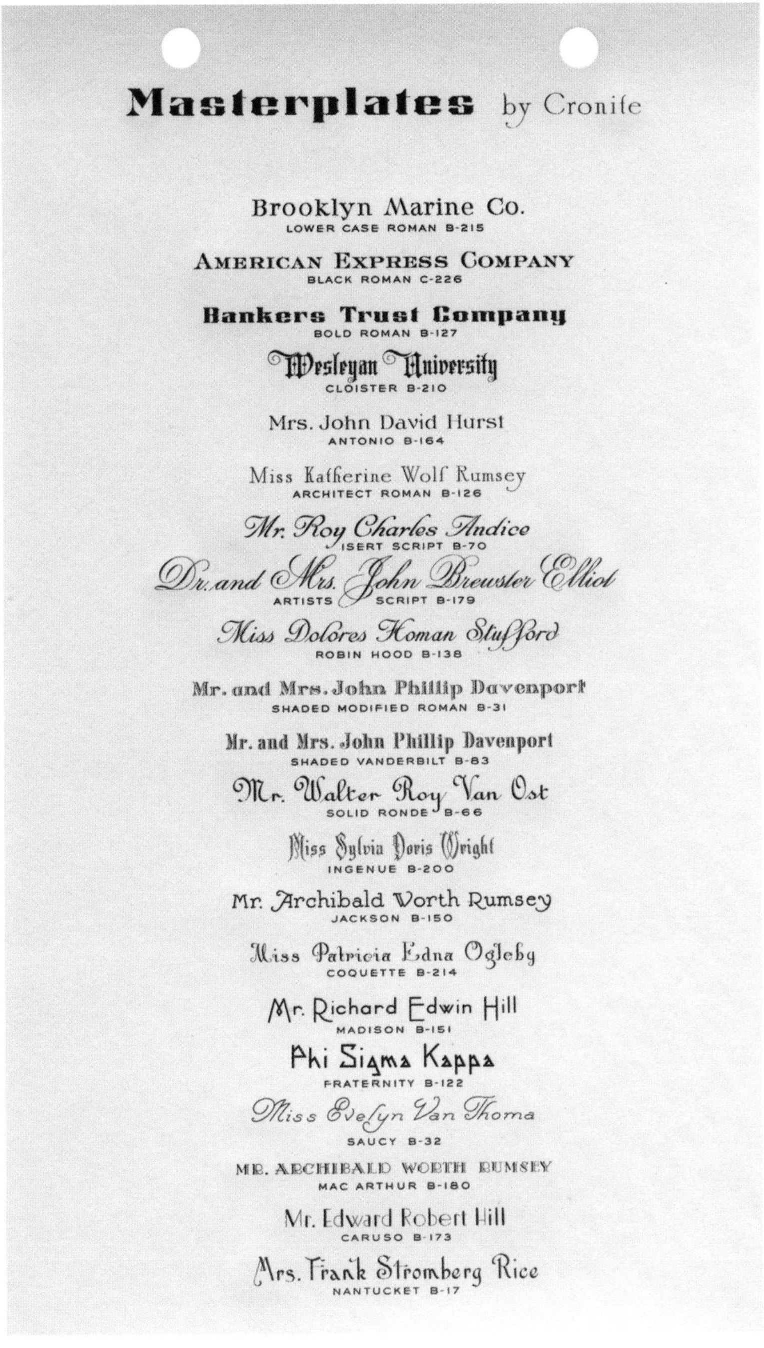

Masterplates by Cronite

Brooklyn Marine Co.
LOWER CASE ROMAN B-215

AMERICAN EXPRESS COMPANY
BLACK ROMAN C-226

Bankers Trust Company
BOLD ROMAN B-127

Wesleyan University
CLOISTER B-210

Mrs. John David Hurst
ANTONIO B-164

Miss Katherine Wolf Rumsey
ARCHITECT ROMAN B-126

Mr. Roy Charles Andice
ISERT SCRIPT B-70

Dr. and Mrs. John Brewster Elliot
ARTISTS SCRIPT B-179

Miss Dolores Homan Stufford
ROBIN HOOD B-138

Mr. and Mrs. John Phillip Davenport
SHADED MODIFIED ROMAN B-31

Mr. and Mrs. John Phillip Davenport
SHADED VANDERBILT B-83

Mr. Walter Roy Van Ost
SOLID RONDE B-66

Miss Sylvia Doris Wright
INGENUE B-200

Mr. Archibald Worth Rumsey
JACKSON B-150

Miss Patricia Edna Oglesby
COQUETTE B-214

Mr. Richard Edwin Hill
MADISON B-151

Phi Sigma Kappa
FRATERNITY B-122

Miss Evelyn Van Thoma
SAUCY B-32

MR. ARCHIBALD WORTH RUMSEY
MAC ARTHUR B-180

Mr. Edward Robert Hill
CARUSO B-173

Mrs. Frank Stromberg Rice
NANTUCKET B-17

MASTERPLATES

Sparks Dental Laboratory
SOLID MODIFIED ROMAN B-41

Lieutenant Cyrus Blackburn
VERGIL B-169

Harris Coal Company
TALLYRAND B-95

MIDTOWN PLUMBING CORP.
PRESTIGE B-211

Libby Owens Ford Co.
DUPONT B-42

BANKERS LUNCHEON CLUB
OUTLINE ROMAN C-207

HYATT BEARINGS CO.
OUTLINED ROMAN B-63

General Service Co.
OUTLINE MODIFIED ROMAN C-205

JOHN ALBERT WARWICK CO.
1 LINE BLOCK NO. 11

JOHN ALBERT WARWICK CO.
2 LINE BLOCK NO. 12

JOHN ALBERT WARWICK CO.
3 LINE BLOCK NO. 13

JOHN ALBERT WARWICK CO.
4 LINE BLOCK NO. 14

JOHN ALBERT WARWICK CO.
5 LINE BLOCK NO. 15

JOHN ALBERT WARWICK CO.
6 LINE BLOCK B-130

JOHN ALBERT WARWICK CO.
MODIFIED GOTHIC B-207

John Albert Warwick Co.
3 LINE LOWER CASE BLOCK B-19

CRONITE CO., Inc.

Masterplate Styles

7

BULOVA WATCH CO.
FORWARD 1 LINE BLOCK NO. C-229

Sun Refrigeration Co.
LOWER CASE SQUARE 2 LINE BLOCK NO. C-227

Sun Refrigeration Co.
MODIFIED STRONGLEY NO. B-152

MOREY BOAT WORKS
2 LINE SLANTED BLOCK NO. B-260

MOREY BOAT WORKS
3 LINE SLANTED BLOCK NO. B-261

MOREY BOAT WORKS
4 LINE SLANTED BLOCK NO. B-262

MOREY'S BOAT WORKS
2 LINE MODIFIED FUTURA NO. B-267

MOREY'S BOAT WORKS
4 LINE MODIFIED FUTURA NO. B-266

MOREY'S BOAT WORKS
6 LINE MODIFIED FUTURA NO. B-265

Doctors Supply Co.
RIBBON NO. B-255

Mr. Emil Clifford Rogers
PARSIFAL NO. C-228

Mr. Emil Clifford Rogers
SLANTED SOL. ANTIQUE ROMAN NO. B-162

Mr. Archibald Worth Rumsey
LOWER CASE ROMAN NO. B-125

Mr. Archibald Worth Rumsey
SLANTED SHADED ANTIQUE ROMAN NO. B 167

Ladies Theatre Guild
SHADED BOLD MODIFIED ROMAN NO. B-48

MR. ARCHIBALD WORTH RUMSEY
SLANTED LIGHT ROMAN NO. B-277

Mr. Frederick Earl Jansen
ANTOIN NO. B-205

HUNG TSAO TEA GARDEN
ALEXANDER NO. B-276

Cronite Co., Inc.

Forward Master Plates
by Cronite

8

ELGIN WATCH COMPANY
FORWARD 1 LINE BLOCK C229

DR. JAMES McDONALD
FORWARD 3 LINE BLOCK C231

NO ADMITTANCE
FORWARD 5 LINE BLOCK C232

REVEREND DWIGHT ALGERNON SMALL
FORWARD CONDENSED 2 LINE BLOCK C233

PLEASE USE ENTRANCE AT REAR
FORWARD CONDENSED 5 LINE BLOCK C225

PHILLIP ANDERSON TAYLOR
FORWARD 3 LINE STRONGLY C234

Grace Moore
FORWARD FILLED-IN SCRIPT C235

ROBERT OLIVER
FORWARD 2 LINE FANCY BLOCK C211

DR. JOHN WILEY
FORWARD LIGHT CLASSIC ROMAN C236

123-123-123-123
WATCH DIAL PLATE C230

PENNSYLVANIA RAILROAD CO.
STYMIE B283

Pennsylvania Railroad Co.
STYMIE LOWER CASE B284

Sullivan and Rothschild
Interior Decorators
CHURCHILL B278

Ecclesiastical Garment Co.
BELGIAN B204

JOHN PARKER KNIGHT
ATTORNEY AT LAW
MORGAN B256

FIRST SECURITIES CORP.
BOLD ROMAN B285

Masterplates

Oriental Rug Company
ORIENTAL B-298

WEST REFRIGERATION CO.
MARSHALL B-64

WEST REFRIGERATION CO.
ROMAN B-158

West Refrigeration Co.
ARCHITECTS LOWER CASE B-75

Mr. John Henry Madison
TRAFTON B-170

Cedar Pottery Guild
PARK AVENUE C-208

Dr. Alston George Shields
SOLID OLD ENGLISH B-140

American Bible Society
ROUSSEAU B-160

Ye Olde Oak Tavern
PICKWICK B-123

Suzelle Millinery Shop
COSSACK B-230

Mrs. Genevieve Hewitt Barclay
WELLINGTON B-80

Miss Gladys Bertha Wright
NIGHTINGALE B-201

Miss Carol Van Nostrand
SOPHISTICATE B-203

MR. SETON HALL BAKER
ROLLY POLLY B-43

Miss Francis Wade Harrison
GLAMOUR B-209

Dr. and Mrs. Walter Pryor Smith
SOCIETY B-251

Mrs. Richard Alice Thompson
HAMILTON B-22

Longchamps Restaurants
LOWER CASE HEAVY ROMAN C-206

Mrs. Harold George Shields
SOLID OLD ENGLISH B-60

Mr. Walter Holmes Shield
RIDLEY'S ROMAN B-317

Cronite Co., Inc.

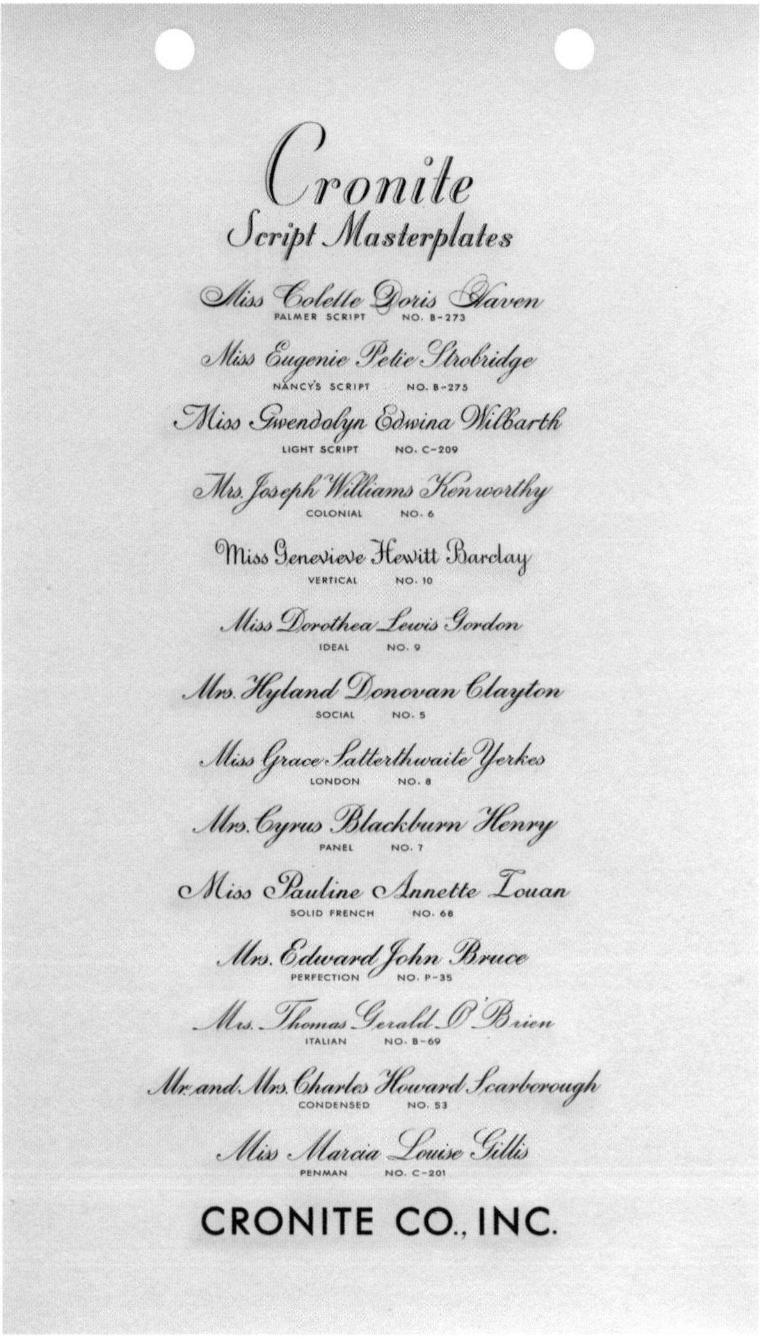

Cronite
Script Masterplates

Miss Colette Doris Haven
PALMER SCRIPT NO. B-273

Miss Eugenie Petie Strobridge
NANCY'S SCRIPT NO. B-275

Miss Gwendolyn Edwina Wilbarth
LIGHT SCRIPT NO. C-209

Mrs. Joseph Williams Kenworthy
COLONIAL NO. 6

Miss Genevieve Hewitt Barclay
VERTICAL NO. 10

Miss Dorothea Lewis Gordon
IDEAL NO. 9

Mrs. Hyland Donovan Clayton
SOCIAL NO. 5

Miss Grace Satterthwaite Yerkes
LONDON NO. 8

Mrs. Cyrus Blackburn Henry
PANEL NO. 7

Miss Pauline Annette Louan
SOLID FRENCH NO. 68

Mrs. Edward John Bruce
PERFECTION NO. P-35

Mrs. Thomas Gerald O'Brien
ITALIAN NO. B-69

Mr. and Mrs. Charles Howard Scarborough
CONDENSED NO. 53

Miss Marcia Louise Gillis
PENMAN NO. C-201

CRONITE CO., INC.

Text Style Masterplates

14

Mrs. Harvey Thomas Ellicot
KENSINGTON NO. B-33

Mrs. Harvey Thomas Ellicot
HAMPSHIRE NO. B-168

Miss Ellen Ruth Smith
CORINTHIAN NO. B-270

Dr. and Mrs. Walter Pryor Smith
ST. JAMES NO. B-250

Mr. and Mrs. Hendrick Loon Stuyvesant
WINDSOR ROYALE NO. 70

Mrs. Percival Allen Quincy
BELVEDERE NO. 63

Miss June Van Nostrand
WESTMINSTER NO. 71

Mr. Harvey Thoma Ellicot
MODIFIED TEXT NO. 34

Dr. and Mrs. Walter Pryor Smith
ST. JAMES NO. 62

Mrs. Robert Edwin Blakely
BAILEY TEXT NO. 19

Miss Sylvia Gwendolyn Petrie
LYNDELL NO. 27

Mr. Tyler Bosworth Hemingway
ANTIQUE TEXT NO. 21

Miss Alice Ruth Kimball
ARTISAN ROMAN NO. 49

Mr. and Mrs. Edward Frank Scholt
ASTOR TEXT NO. B-56

MR. JOHN KREW BARRYMORE
BLOCK TEXT NO. B-23

Mr. Tyler Bosworth Hemingway
ANTIQUE TEXT NO. B-216

MR. HORACE JOHN BILTSHIRE
ROMAN TEXT NO. B-178

CRONITE CO., INC.

TEXT MASTERPLATES

15

Mr. Walter Allen Jones
VERTEAQUE TEXT C-65

Mrs. George Carl Elliot
NORMAN TEXT C-214

Miss Alice King Parson
LAFAYETTE TEXT C-213

Mr. and Mrs. Frank Knight Worth
MASONIC TEXT C-215

Mrs. Mary Edith Cornell
CATHEDRAL TEXT C-212

MR. ROBERT HILL SPEARS
ROMAN TEXT C-221

Miss Grace Ottley Van Dyke
OLD ENGLISH TEXT C-217

Mrs. Peter Roy Burgess
LUCERNE TEXT C-219

Miss Vera Clews Thornton
CAXTON TEXT C-218

Miss Margaret Claire Rymer
SPANISH TEXT C-220

Miss Doris Penny Crocker
RONDE TEXT C-216

Miss Genevieve Doris Barclay
SHADED LUCERNE B-14

Miss Carol June Towne
SHADED OLD ENGLISH B-40

Mrs. John David Hurst
SHADED BONAPARTE B-29

Miss Patsy Flemington
SHADED CAROL B-50

HUNT PARKS ASSN.
SHADED ARCHITECT ROMAN B-36

Mrs. Tyler Duke Boswell
SHADED CROMWELL B-49

Miss Elizabeth Van Nostrand
SHADED WELCH B-161

Mr. Robert Wilson Mather
SHADED RECTANGULAR C-210

CRONITE CO., INC.

Shaded Style Sheet No. 1

Mr. and Mrs. Peter Allen Stuart
SHADED OLD ENGLISH NO. B-37

Mr. Chandler Darrell Spears
SHADED ROMAN NO. B-187

Dr. and Mrs. George Rodney Stuart
SHADED ANTIQUE ROMAN NO. 20

Miss Vera Clews Thornton
SHADED ANTIQUE ROMAN NO. B-26

Mr. and Mrs. Allen Percy Duncan
ANTIQUE TEXT NO. 21

Mr. and Mrs. Peter Roy Burgess
SHADED CAXTON NO. 36

Miss Margaret Claire Rymer
SHADED SPANISH NO. 33

Mr. Oliver Simms Lyons
SHADED NORMAN NO. 48

Miss Grace Ottley Van Dyke
SHADED RONDE NO. 50

Mr. and Mrs. James Fay Cunningham
SHADED CATHEDRAL NO. 64

Mr. Robert Hills Mansfield
SHADED VERTEAQUE NO. 65

Mrs. Mary Edith Cornell
SHADED BLACKSTONE NO. 66

Mr. and Mrs. John Phillip Davenport
SHADED MODIFIED ROMAN NO. 73

Mr. Chandler Darrell Spears
SHADED ROMAN NO. 38

Mr. Chandler Darrell Spears
SHADED ROMAN NO. B-58

Mr. and Mrs. Frank Knight Worth
SHADED MASONIC NO. B-135

Cronite Co., Inc.

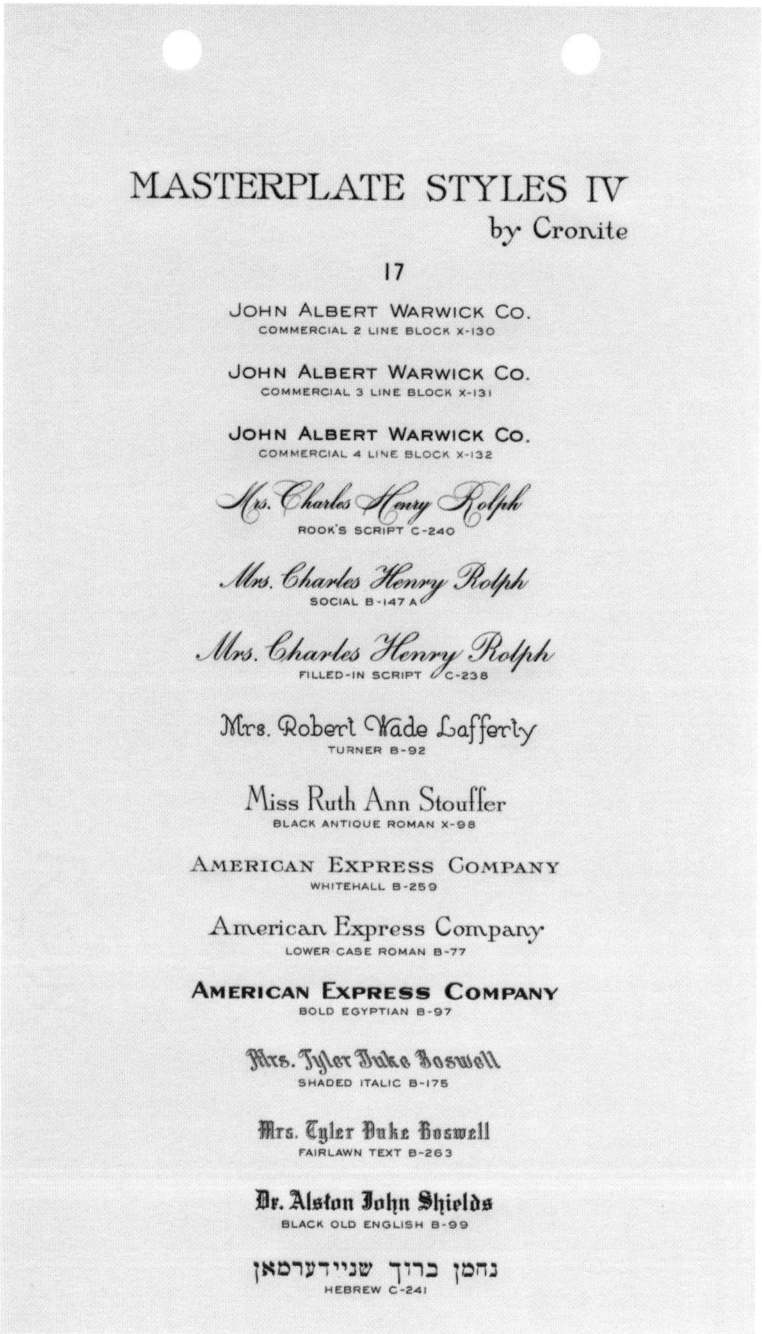

MASTERPLATE STYLES IV

by Cronite

17

JOHN ALBERT WARWICK CO.
COMMERCIAL 2 LINE BLOCK X-130

JOHN ALBERT WARWICK CO.
COMMERCIAL 3 LINE BLOCK X-131

JOHN ALBERT WARWICK CO.
COMMERCIAL 4 LINE BLOCK X-132

Mrs. Charles Henry Rolph
ROOK'S SCRIPT C-240

Mrs. Charles Henry Rolph
SOCIAL B-147 A

Mrs. Charles Henry Rolph
FILLED-IN SCRIPT C-238

Mrs. Robert Wade Lafferty
TURNER B-92

Miss Ruth Ann Stouffer
BLACK ANTIQUE ROMAN X-98

AMERICAN EXPRESS COMPANY
WHITEHALL B-259

American Express Company
LOWER CASE ROMAN B-77

AMERICAN EXPRESS COMPANY
BOLD EGYPTIAN B-97

Mrs. Tyler Duke Boswell
SHADED ITALIC B-175

Mrs. Tyler Duke Boswell
FAIRLAWN TEXT B-263

Dr. Alston John Shields
BLACK OLD ENGLISH B-99

נחמן ברוך שניידערמאן
HEBREW C-241

Sun Luck Restaurant

ORIENTAL B 298

Mrs. Robert Smith requests the honour

RIDLEY'S ROMAN B 317

PENNSYLVANIA Railroad Company

SL. LOWER CASE ROMAN B 322

Western Manufacturing Company

LOWER CASE ROMAN B 316

First National City Bank

CONDENSED ROMAN B 321

Bowery Savings Bank

LOWER CASE ROMAN B 308

SUN REFRIGERATION CO.

JENNER'S ROMAN B 325

AMERICAN LAWN EQUIPMENT COMPANY

4 LINE CONDENSED BLOCK B 304

JOHN GRANT SMITH VICE PRESIDENT

2 LINE CONDENSED BLOCK B 305

Warner & Swasey Company

LOWER CASE ROMAN B 310

RICHARD OGLEBY Vice President

SLANTED ROMAN B 318

Remington Arms Company

SLANTED 2 LINE BLOCK B 306

CLYDE SANDBURY Adjustment Supervisor

3 LINE FUTURA B 302

Prudential Insurance Company

LOWER CASE ROMAN B 309

Mrs. Thomas Stanley O'Brien

ANGULAR SCRIPT C 244

CRONITE

1973 MASTERPLATE STYLES

19

General Manufacturing Company

2 LINE HELVETICA LIGHT NO. B 347

General Manufacturing Company

3 LINE HELVETICA NORMAL NO. B 338

General Manufacturing Company

4 LINE HELVETICA MEDIUM NO. B 327

General Manufacturing Company

6 LINE HELVETICA BOLD NO. B 349

General Manufacturing Company

5 LINE HELVETICA EXTRA BOLD NO. B 350

METROPOLITAN CONSTRUCTION CORP.

2 LINE HELVETICA COND. NO. B 335

METROPOLITAN CONSTRUCTION CORP.

3 LINE HELVETICA NO. B 339

METROPOLITAN CONSTRUCTION CORP.

4 LINE HELVETICA COND. NO. B 348

Lawrence Shipping Corp.

2 LINE UNIVERS NO. B 353

Lawrence Shipping Corp.

4 LINE UNIVERS NO. B 352

Liberty Motors Company

2 LINE UNIVERS COND. NO. B 329

Liberty Motors Company

4 LINE UNIVERS COND. NO. B 328

V. P. HALPIN CORPORATION

CORVINUS NO. B 296

CRONITE

1973 MASTERPLATE STYLES II

20

ELECTRONIC DESIGN COMPANY
2 LINE MICROGRAMMA B 331

ELECTRONIC DESIGN COMPANY
4 LINE MICROGRAMMA B 332

ELECTRONIC DESIGN COMPANY
6 LINE MICROGRAMMA B 333

LEONARD THOMAS HEMINGWAY
EXTRA THIN ROMAN B 320

Martin J. Hollingsworth
SERLIO ROMAN B 326

AMERICAN MFG COMPANY
HEAVY ROMAN B 336

Republic Trust Company
2 LINE EUROSTYLE B 344

Republic Trust Company
3 LINE EUROSTYLE B 345

Republic Trust Company
4 LINE EUROSTYLE B 346

American Lighting Company
OPTIMA C 248

GENERAL MANUFACTURING COMPANY
2 LINE SMALL HELVETICA B 340

Mr. and Mrs. John G. Sullivan
ENGLISH SCRIPT C 247

CRONITE

1977 MASTERPLATE STYLES

21

General Manufacturing Company

2 LINE SLANTED HELVETICA NO. B 342

General Manufacturing Company

4 LINE SLANTED HELVETICA NO. B 343

GENERAL MANUFACTURING COMPANY

STRONGLEY NO. B 312

General Manufacturing Company

4 LINE FUTURA NO. B 292

General Manufacturing Company

3 LINE EURO-STYLE COND. NO. B 355

GENERAL MANUFACTURING COMPANY

ANTONIO NO. B 165

General Manufacturing Company

CASLON NO. B 90

General Manufacturing Company

IMPRESSUM COND. B 354

GENERAL MANUFACTURING COMPANY

NEW NARROW ROMAN B 290

GENERAL MANUFACTURING COMPANY

SOL. ROMAN B 264

General Manufacturing Company

CATHEDRAL SCRIPT NO. B 299

General Manufacturing Company

COLONIAL SCRIPT NO. B 188

General Manufacturing Company

BLACK OLD ENGLISH NO. B 196

General Manufacturing Company

SHADED ANTHENIAN NO. B 39

KEY TO MASTERPLATE STYLES

p.169: *Engravers Letter Styles* is a sample book of styles in the Cronite Masterplate system, published by the Cronite Company, North Bergen, New Jersey, probably dating from before the 1970s. The title is engraved on copper metallic cover stock bound with brads, and the book is unpaginated. Pages contain Roman, italic, sans serif, decorative and traditional script, as well as idiosyncratic vintage styles, primarily for display.

p.171: Sample page showing decorative scripts, an interesting Arthurian-like style (Cloister B210), and a couple of shaded styles.

p.172: Sample page including six different Line Block styles. Notice there are uppercase characters only, no lowercase.

p.173: Sample page showing Bulova (top) backward, because the styles engrave right-reading on clocks, knives, and firearms. Also shown here is Morey's Boat Works, a wonderful and curious riff on early to mid-twentieth-century type specimens. In typographic circles, styles designated as "slanted" are just that—slanted. There is a slanting feature on some pantograph machines—rather than a true italic.

p.174: Sample page including Ecclesiastical Garment Co., which appears to date from the Aesthetic Movement. Others are engraver's translations of familiar typography developed through the letterpress tradition, such as the slab serif Stymie, originally designed by Morris Fuller Benton in 1931.

p.175: Sample page including two different examples of Old English, other styles inspired by blackletter, and one of the author's favorites, Glamour B-209.

p.176: Sample page of some lovely scripts that show off the delicate, thin strokes and the graceful swells indicative of hand engraving.

p.177: Sample page showing Roman Text No. B-178, a current favorite of those in the socialite set.

p.178: Sample page showing shaded versions of blackletter (or Old English), where many lines are used to achieve the appearance of shading.

p.179: Sample page with more shaded and Old English-like styles.

p.180: Sample page including three more Line Block specimens.

p.181: Sample page with an interesting version of Futura, 3 Line Futura B 302. "3 Line" refers to the thickness of the stroke, "1" being the thinnest.

p.182: Sample page by Eaton (Sag Harbor, New York, acquired by the Cronite Company in 1974) showing cuts of Helvetica and Univers, which look strange as engraver's lettering.

p.183: Sample page by Eaton showing more mid-twentieth-century type styles.

p.184: Sample page with "Slanted Helvetica," which has literally been stretched into a slant and is not a true italic.

APPENDIX

B

NEW ENGRAVER'S FONTS BY MONOTYPE IMAGING

For the launch of this book, Monotype Imaging Corporation, a font-developing company specializing in custom typeface design and font technology, developed two new fonts that are based on Cronite Masterplate engraving styles—JMC Engraver (based on Gaston) [**Figs. 1, 4**] and Feldman Engraver (based on Pendleton) [**Figs. 2, 4**]—and are available for free download with the purchase of this book.[1] The original Masterplate styles collection was compiled in the 1950s or 1960s (see appendix A for examples) by Robert N. Steffens, son of Cronite Company's founder, Frank Steffens. In 1974 Robert Steffens purchased the Library of Engravers Styles by Eaton, of Sag Harbor, New York, making Cronite's pantograph library the most complete anywhere.

Complete Masterplate character sets exist only as metal templates, or Masterplates, so there is no way to see all the letters, numerals, and punctuation of a specific type style without having them engraved. To digitize the Masterplate character styles, several steps were involved: Engraver Tommy Flax, who has engraved plates and dies for me since 1984, graciously donated his time and steel plates, engraving a type specimen page for both styles using the Cronite Masterplate system. In addition, Emily DeLorge engraved glyphs and ligatures for the project to maintain some of the idiosyncrasies of engraved typography. Art Scroll Printing, in New York, then ran press proofs from the plates. [**Figs. 3, 8, 11**] Creative Type Director Steve Matteson did the initial digital conversion from scans of the press proofs [**Figs. 5, 7**], and Terrance Weinzierl added to the characters in Fontlab, turning strokes into outline, modifying the letterforms to appear happily together as one typeface, and specifying sidebearings, the space built into the left and right side of each character. [**Figs. 9, 10**] The following pages illustrate some of the steps involved in digitizing the two engravers' lettering styles.

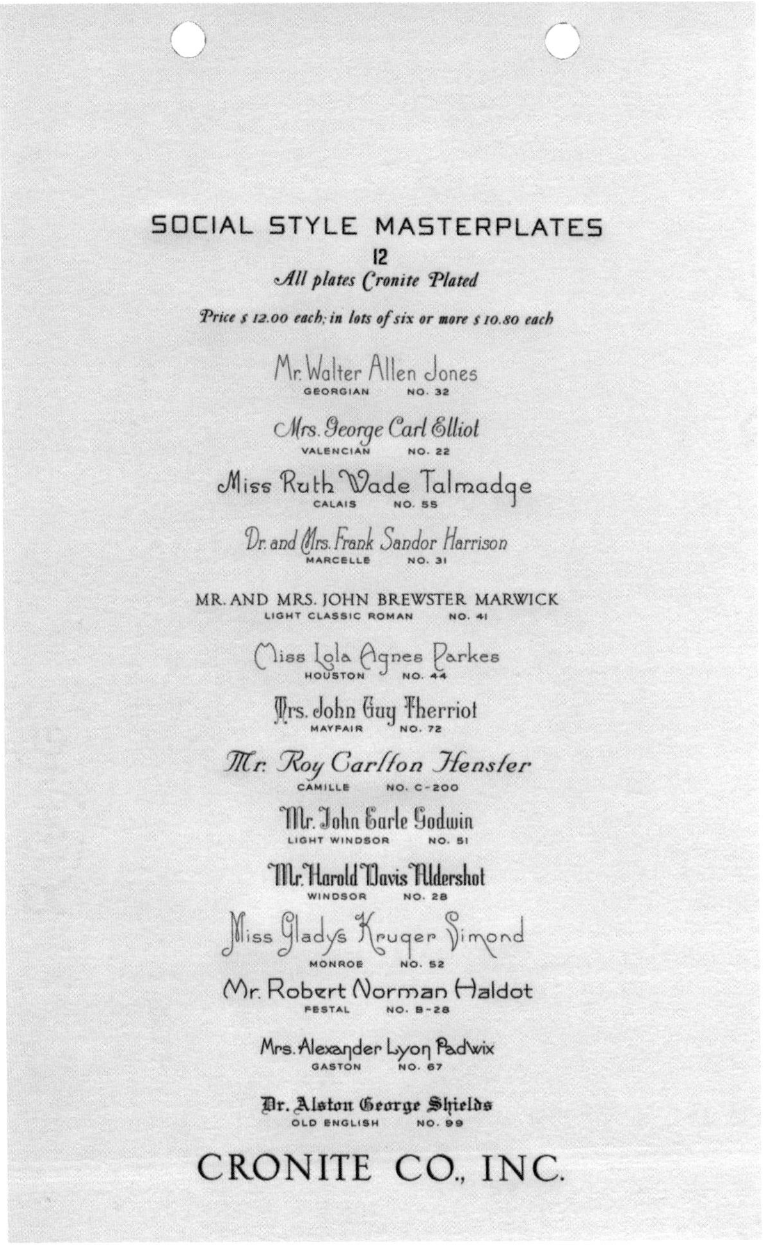

SOCIAL STYLE MASTERPLATES

12

All plates Cronite Plated

Price $ 12.00 each; in lots of six or more $ 10.80 each

Mr. Walter Allen Jones
GEORGIAN NO. 32

Mrs. George Carl Elliot
VALENCIAN NO. 22

Miss Ruth Wade Talmadge
CALAIS NO. 55

Dr. and Mrs. Frank Sandor Harrison
MARCELLE NO. 31

MR. AND MRS. JOHN BREWSTER MARWICK
LIGHT CLASSIC ROMAN NO. 41

Miss Lola Agnes Parkes
HOUSTON NO. 44

Mrs. John Guy Therriot
MAYFAIR NO. 72

Mr. Roy Carlton Hensler
CAMILLE NO. C-200

Mr. John Earle Godwin
LIGHT WINDSOR NO. 51

Mr. Harold Davis Aldershot
WINDSOR NO. 28

Miss Gladys Kruger Simond
MONROE NO. 52

Mr. Robert Norman Haldot
FESTAL NO. B-28

Mrs. Alexander Lyon Padwix
GASTON NO. 67

Dr. Alston George Shields
OLD ENGLISH NO. 99

CRONITE CO., INC.

Fig. 1: Sample page from the Cronite Masterplate catalog, showing Gaston No. 67, among other styles, on which JMC Engraver is based.

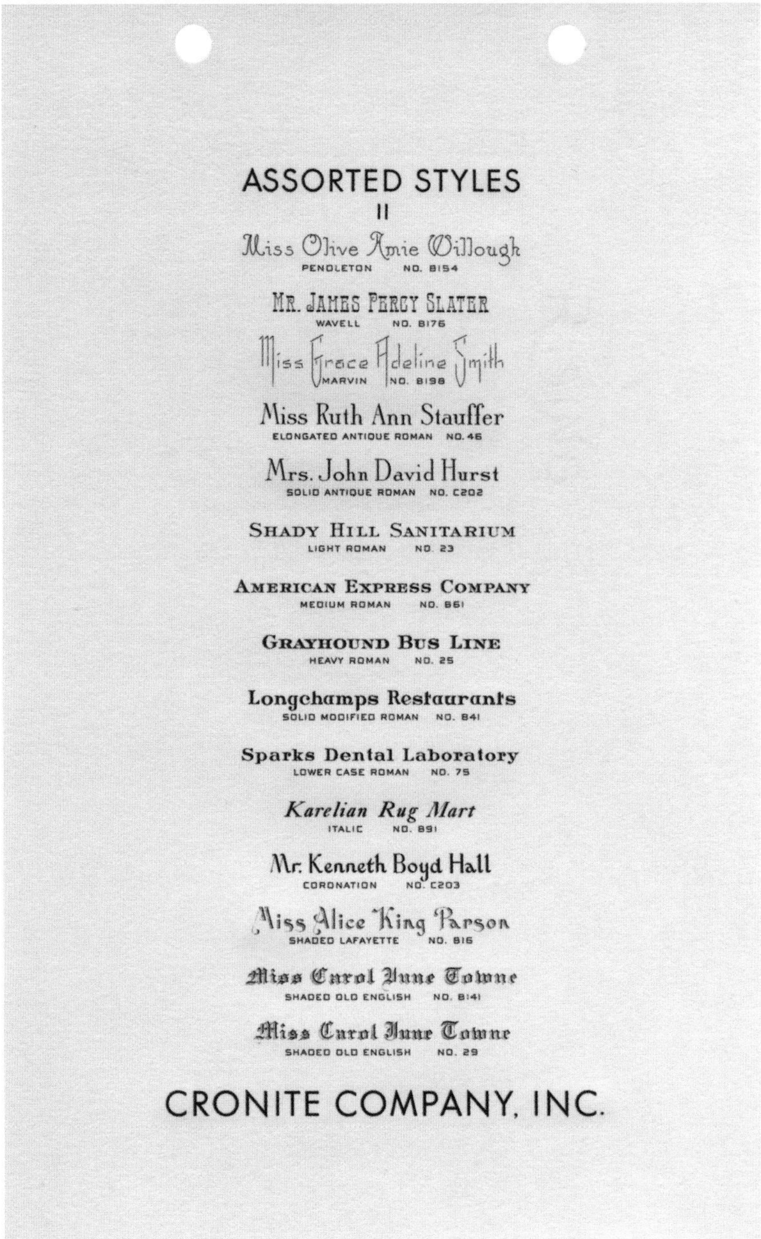
ASSORTED STYLES
II
Miss Olive Amie Willough
PENDLETON NO. B154
MR. JAMES PERCY SLATER
WAVELL NO. B176
Miss Grace Adeline Smith
MARVIN NO. B198
Miss Ruth Ann Stauffer
ELONGATED ANTIQUE ROMAN NO. 46
Mrs. John David Hurst
SOLID ANTIQUE ROMAN NO. C202
SHADY HILL SANITARIUM
LIGHT ROMAN NO. 23
AMERICAN EXPRESS COMPANY
MEDIUM ROMAN NO. B61
GRAYHOUND BUS LINE
HEAVY ROMAN NO. 25
Longchamps Restaurants
SOLID MODIFIED ROMAN NO. B41
Sparks Dental Laboratory
LOWER CASE ROMAN NO. 75
Karelian Rug Mart
ITALIC NO. B91
Mr. Kenneth Boyd Hall
CORONATION NO. C203
Miss Alice King Parson
SHADED LAFAYETTE NO. B16
Miss Carol June Towne
SHADED OLD ENGLISH NO. B141
Miss Carol June Towne
SHADED OLD ENGLISH NO. 29
CRONITE COMPANY, INC.

Fig. 2: Sample page showing Pendelton No. B154, among others, which was the inspiration for Feldman Engraver.

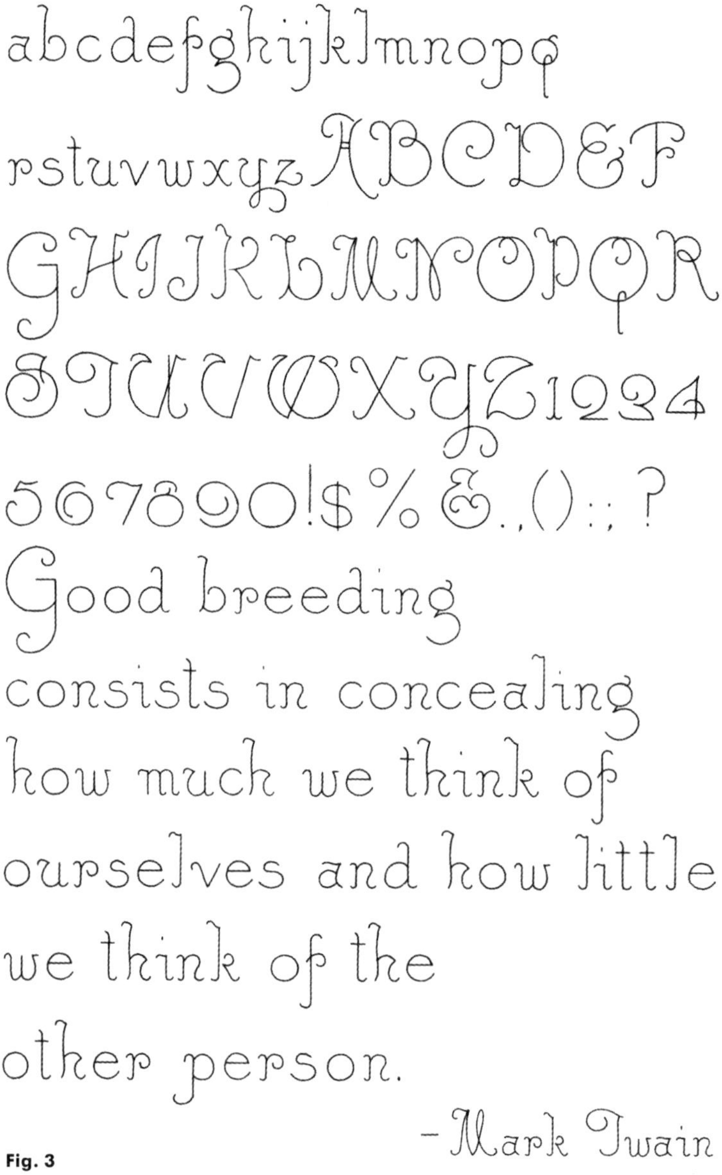
abcdefghijklmnopq
rstuvwxyzABCDEF
GHIJKLMNOPQR
STUVWXYZ1234
567890!$%&.,():;?
Good breeding
consists in concealing
how much we think of
ourselves and how little
we think of the
other person.
-Mark Twain

Fig. 3
Press proof of specimen pages engraved for this project (Pendleton, above, and Gaston, opposite).

abcdefghijklmnopq
rstuvwxyzABCDEF
GHIJKLMNOPQR
STUVWXYZ1234
567890!$%&.,():;?

"Good breeding
consists in concealing
how much we think of
ourselves and how little
we think of the
other person."

—Mark Twain

Mrs. Alexander Lyon Padwix
GASTON NO. 67
Miss Olive Amie Willough
PENDLETON NO. B154

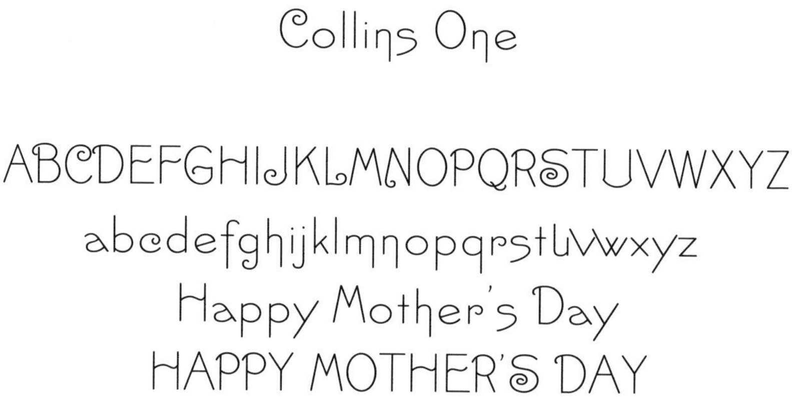
Collins One
ABCDEFGHIJKLMNOPQRSTUVWXYZ
abcdefghijklmnopqrstuvwxyz
Happy Mother's Day
HAPPY MOTHER'S DAY

Fig. 4, top and middle: Close-up specimens of the original Masterplate Engraved Styles, Gaston No. 67 and Pendelton No. B154.

Fig. 5, bottom: Original digital version of Gaston by Steve Matteson.

Fig. 6, opposite top, left to right: Uppercase *N* from original scan of the Pendelton press proof; auto-traced *N* in Adobe Illustrator to produce initial outlines; smoothed and developed letter.

Fig. 7, opposite bottom: Initial digital conversion of Gaston.

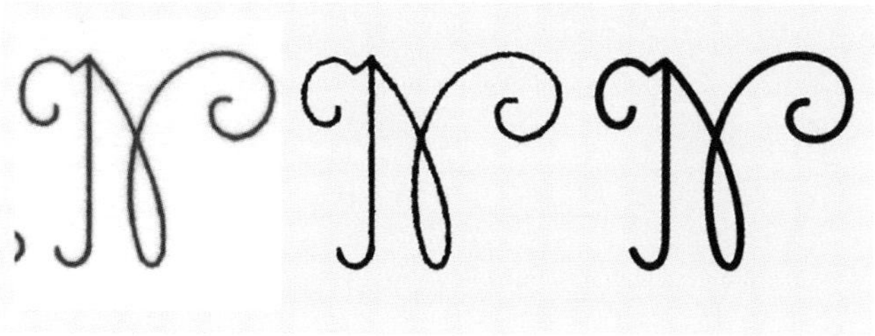

Five quacking zephyrs jolt my wax bed.

0123456789

Wonder Omlet

Wonder Omlet

Fifth Shushi Check

final soft fluff stifle

FIVE QUACKING ZEPHYRS

JOLT MY WAX BED

Collin's Engraver

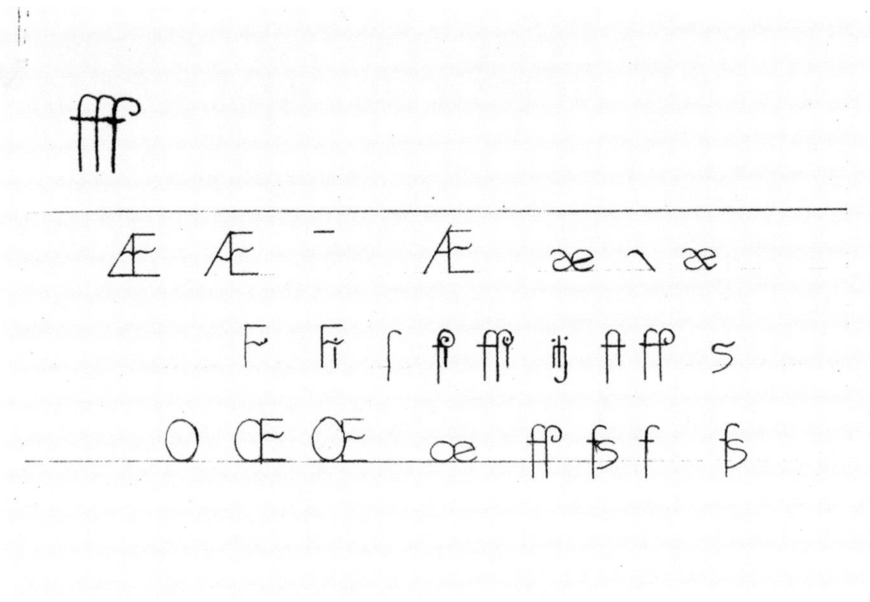

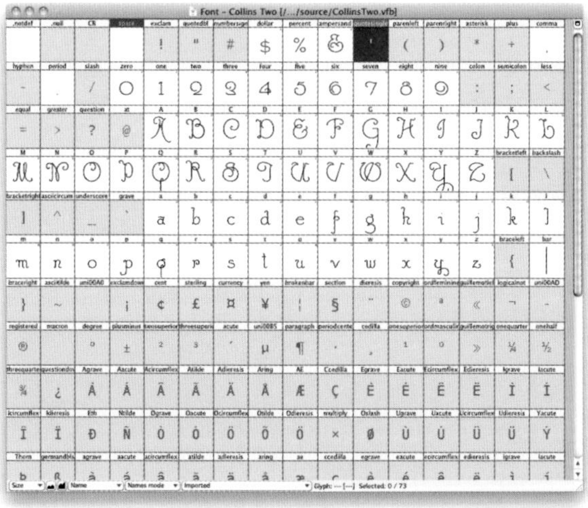
Font – Collins Two [/.../source/CollinsTwo.vfb]

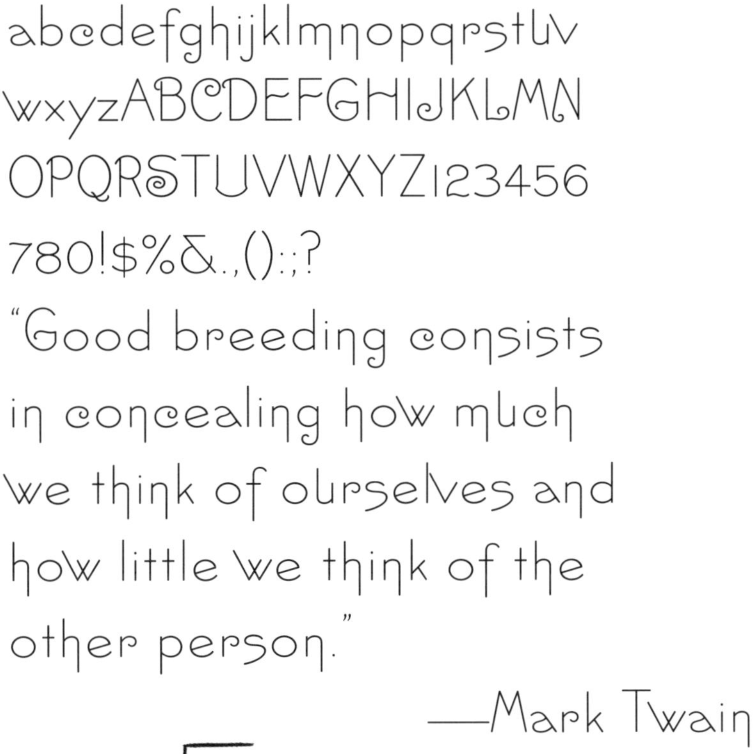
abcdefghijklmnopqrstuv
wxyzABCDEFGHIJKLMN
OPQRSTUVWXYZ123456
780!$%&.,():;?
"Good breeding consists
in concealing how much
we think of ourselves and
how little we think of the
other person."
—Mark Twain

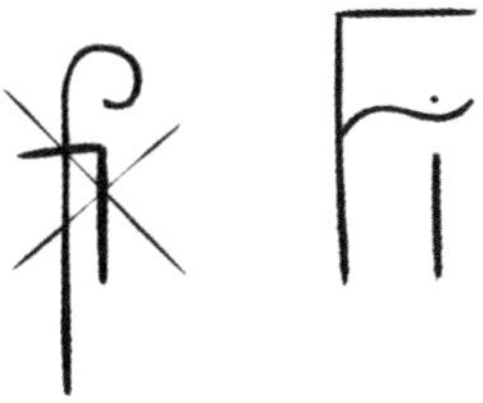

Fig. 8, opposite, top: Some of DeLorge's ligatures.

Fig. 9, opposite, bottom: A first-draft character set (shown here as a screen shot), also includes some of the international language accent marks and diacritics developed for Pendleton.

Fig. 10, top: Preliminary type specimen page set with an early version of JMC Engraver.

Fig. 11, bottom: Detail of a press proof of an engraved ligature showing terminals (where the burin or graver enters and exits a cut).

GLOSSARY

AT HOME CARD: A CARD SENT TO FAMILY AND FRIENDS ANNOUNCING THAT YOU HAVE MOVED AND GIVING YOUR NEW ADDRESS AND CONTACT INFORMATION. IN FORMER TIMES, IT WAS USED AS AN ANNOUNCEMENT THAT THE SENDER WOULD BE RECEIVING (AT THAT ADDRESS).

BÉZIER CURVES: SMOOTH CURVES BASED ON POINTS CONNECTING LINES THAT ARC IN VECTOR-BASED SOFTWARE. IN PROGRAMS SUCH AS ADOBE'S ILLUSTRATOR AND FREEHAND, THESE CAN BE COMBINED TO FORM COMPLEX CURVES AND SHAPES THAT SCALE PERFECTLY AND ARE COMPATIBLE WITH MOST PREPRESS FUNCTIONS IN THE ENGRAVED STATIONERY INDUSTRY.

BLACKLETTER: TYPEFACES AND LETTERFORMS, SUCH AS OLD ENGLISH, THAT APPEAR GOTHIC AND LOOK LIKE MEDIEVAL-STYLE CALLIGRAPHY. THE TYPE FOR GUTENBERG'S 42-LINE BIBLE WAS SET IN BLACKLETTER.

BRUISE: IMPRESSION ON THE BACK OF AN ENGRAVED PIECE OF STATIONERY.

BURIN: TOOL USED TO ENGRAVE PLATES AND DIES, ALSO CALLED A GRAVER.

BURR: METAL CUT UP FROM THE SURFACE OF A METAL PLATE OR DIE WHILE ENGRAVING.

CALLING CARD: A SMALL CARD USED TO ANNOUNCE A CALLER'S PRESENCE OR TO BE REMEMBERED BY IN POLITE SOCIETY. USUALLY IT HAS THE BEARER'S NAME ONLY. TODAY, CALLING CARDS ARE INCREASINGLY EXCHANGED SOCIALLY IN LIEU OF BUSINESS CARDS.

CANARY PAPER: A KIND OF TRACING PAPER, SOMETIMES YELLOWISH IN COLOR.

CHASE: IN LETTERPRESS PRINTING, THE FRAME IN WHICH THE INDIVIDUAL PIECES OF TYPE ARE ASSEMBLED (COMPOSED) INTO A PAGE LAYOUT OR A DESIGN.

CHINESE WHITE: WATER-SOLUBLE, OPAQUE WHITE PIGMENT CONSISTING OF ZINC OXIDE THAT CAN BE APPLIED TO A PLATE OR DIE TO MAKE THE SURFACE RECEPTIVE TO DRAWING. ALSO USED IN WATERCOLOR PAINTING.

CIPHER: A DESIGN BASED ON AN ARRANGEMENT OF INITIALS. UNLIKE A TRUE MONOGRAM, THE INDIVIDUAL LETTERS DO NOT HAVE TO CONNECT OR EVEN TOUCH. MANY SO-CALLED MONOGRAMS TODAY ARE ACTUALLY CIPHERS.

COCKLE: A PUCKERED FINISH AVAILABLE AS AN ALTERNATIVE TO SMOOTH-SURFACED ONIONSKIN PAPER.

COPPERPLATE ENGRAVING: LETTERS, ART, OR DESIGNS CUT INTO A SHEET OF COPPER FOR THE PURPOSE OF MAKING A PRINT.

COUNTER: PAPERBOARD CUT TO THE APPROXIMATE SIZE AND SHAPE OF AN ENGRAVED PLATE OR DIE USED IN DIE STAMPING. THE COUNTER HELPS AVOID SPITTING (INK GOING OUTSIDE OF THE IMPRESSION). COUNTERS CAN ALSO BE MOLDED FROM POLYMER.

DEBOSS: A DESIGN THAT IS IMPRESSED BELOW THE PAPER SURFACE. SEE *EMBOSS*.

DIE: THE MATRIX UPON WHICH AN ENGRAVING IS MADE. USUALLY MADE OUT OF STEEL AND THICKER THAN PLATES; ABOUT HALF AN INCH IS THE NORM. SEE ALSO *PLATE*.

DIE STAMPING PRESS: A PRINTING PRESS USED TO STAMP AN ENGRAVED PLATE OR DIE ONTO PAPER, LEAVING AN INKED IMPRESSION, OR PRINT.

EMBOSS: A DESIGN THAT IS RAISED ABOVE THE PAPER SURFACE. ENGRAVED STATIONERY APPEARS EMBOSSED BECAUSE THE INK IS LITERALLY PUSHED UP ABOVE THE SURFACE OF THE PAPER. A BLIND EMBOSS IS A RAISED IMPRESSION MADE WITHOUT INK.

ENGRAVE: THE ACT OF CUTTING WORDS OR PICTURES INTO METAL (OR WOOD) TO MAKE A SERIES OF (NEARLY IDENTICAL) PRINTS. CHARACTERISTIC OF AN ENGRAVED PIECE OF STATIONERY IS A RAISED INK SURFACE, WITH AN INDENTATION, OR BRUISE, ON THE BACK. ENGRAVING IS AN INTAGLIO PROCESS, WHEREAS LETTERPRESS PRINTING IS A RELIEF PROCESS.

FAMILY CREST: ONE ELEMENT IN A COAT OF ARMS, USUALLY A SYMBOLIC ICON, SUCH AS A LION, A STAG, OR A BEEHIVE. IT COMES FROM THE EUROPEAN HERALDIC TRADITION.

FAMILY SEAL: USUALLY EMBOSSED, MAY SHARE ELEMENTS OF A COAT OF ARMS, BUT IS NOT NECESSARILY RELATED TO HERALDRY.

FIRST DAY COVER: AN ENVELOPE FRANKED WITH A NEWLY ISSUED POSTAGE STAMP, BEARING THE POSTMARK OF THE FIRST DAY OF ISSUE AND AN OFFICIALLY CHOSEN PLACE OF ISSUE.

FORCE: THE THICK METAL SHAFT ON A DIE STAMPING PRESS THAT CONVEYS THE EXTREME PRESSURE NECESSARY DURING DIE STAMPING PRINTING.

GRAVER: TOOL USED TO ENGRAVE PLATES AND DIES, ALSO CALLED A BURIN.

INTAGLIO: AN ENGRAVING, CUTTING, ETCHING, INCISING, OR SCRATCHING INTO THE SURFACE OF A PLATE OR DIE. IN INTAGLIO PRINTING, THE INCISED AREAS ARE INKED AND MADE INTO A PRINT OR SERIES OF PRINTS.

LETTERPRESS PRINTING: ORIGINALLY, THE PRINTING PROCESS BY WHICH RAISED LETTERFORMS ON INDIVIDUAL BLOCKS OF METAL WERE ORGANIZED INTO WORDS, SENTENCES, AND BLOCKS OF TEXT IN A CHASE FOR INKING AND PRINTING. JOHANNES GUTENBERG IS WIDELY ACCEPTED AS HAVING PERFECTED THIS SYSTEM OF MOVABLE TYPE THAT COULD BE ASSEMBLED AND DISASSEMBLED, ALLOWING THE TYPE TO BE USED OVER AND OVER. CHARACTERISTIC OF A LETTERPRESS PRINTING IS THAT THE INK IS DEBOSSED INTO THE SURFACE OF THE PAPER. CONTEMPORARY LETTERPRESS PRINTING RARELY RELIES ON INDIVIDUAL PIECES OF TYPE ANYMORE; A POLYMER PLATE IS CREATED INSTEAD, USUALLY FROM DIGITAL FILES. LETTERPRESS IS A RELIEF PRINTING PROCESS.

LETTER PAPERS: SEE *SOCIAL STATIONERY.*

LETTER SHEET: TRADITIONAL STATIONERY PAPER RARELY USED TODAY. THE OVERSIZED SHEET QUARTER-FOLDED IN A MANNER STILL SEEN IN FORMAL WEDDING INVITATIONS. THE SHEET, FOLDED ONCE HORIZONTALLY AND ONCE VERTICALLY, PRODUCES FOUR PAGES FOR WRITING.

LINE ART: A PREDIGITAL GRAPHIC ART TERM MEANING BLACK-AND-WHITE ART, PREPARED FOR COMMERCIAL REPRODUCTION. IN THE COMPUTER SOFTWARE VERNACULAR, LINE ART IS VECTOR ART OR SPOT COLOR. IT IS 100 PERCENT BLACK, MADE UP OF SOLID BLACK PIXELS (IF IT IS RASTER-BASED ART), OR A STROKED POINT, LINE, CLOSED PATH, OR OBJECT (IF IT IS VECTOR BASED).

LINE ENGRAVING: IN PRINTMAKING, A COMBINATION OF ETCHING AND ENGRAVING, WITH BOTH PROCESSES UTILIZED TO THEIR BEST ADVANTAGE TO ACHIEVE GREATEST DETAIL.

LITHOGRAPHY (OR PLANOGRAPHIC PRINTING): NEITHER A RELIEF NOR INTAGLIO PRINTING PROCESS. THE PRINTING SURFACE AND RESULTING PRINT IN LITHOGRAPHY ARE FLAT. A DESIGN IS DRAWN ONTO A LITHOGRAPHIC SURFACE (ORIGINALLY A THICK SLAB OF LIMESTONE) WITH OIL-BASED INK OR CRAYON. A SERIES OF CHEMICALS HELPS THE SURFACE REPEL WATER WHERE THE OIL MEDIUM HAS BEEN APPLIED AND TO HOLD WATER WHERE IT HAS NOT. IN THE PRINTING PROCESS, INK STICKS TO THE OILY AREAS AND IS THEN TRANSFERRED TO PAPER, REPLICATING, IN REVERSE, THE ORIGINAL DRAWING. INNOVATIONS IN THE PROCESS INCLUDE CHROMOLITHOGRAPHY, CREATING

FULL-COLOR IMAGERY, AND OFFSET LITHOGRAPHY, PRODUCING HUNDREDS AND THOUSANDS OF PRINTS FROM THE SAME ORIGINALS.

MAKEREADY: ALL PROCESSES NECESSARY TO PREPARE A PRESS FOR PRINTING.

MATRIX: AN OBJECT UPON WHICH A DESIGN IS MADE FOR THE PURPOSE OF PRODUCING MULTIPLE PRINTS, SUCH AS A METAL PLATE OR DIE; A WOOD BLOCK; A LITHOGRAPHY STONE; OR EVEN A POTATO, AN ERASER, OR A RUBBER STAMP.

MONARCH SHEET: A SPECIFIC SIZE OF COMMERCIAL STATIONERY (7¼ BY 10½ INCHES) THAT, WHEN FOLDED TWICE, FITS INSIDE A MONARCH ENVELOPE.

MONOGRAM: A DESIGN MADE WITH INTERLOCKING INITIALS IN WHICH THE STRUCTURE OF EACH IS DEPENDENT ON A MAIN PIECE OF EACH OF THE OTHER LETTERS. IF THE INDIVIDUAL LETTERS IN A MONOGRAM WERE SEPARATED, THEY WOULD NOT BE READABLE AS THE LETTERS THEY REPRESENT WHEN INTERTWINED.

OFFSET: THE UNFORTUNATE EFFECT OF INK THAT HAS NOT DRIED WITHIN A STACK OF PRINTED SHEETS AND RUBS OFF ON THE BACK OF THE SHEET ON TOP OF IT.

OLD STYLE: TYPEFACES ORIGINATING PRIMARILY FROM THE 1500S TO 1700S, SUCH AS GOUDY, PERPETUA, SABON, AND CASLON. OLD STYLE TYPEFACES HAVE MORE CONTRAST BETWEEN THICK AND THIN STROKES AND A MORE UPRIGHT STRESS (OR SLANT) THAN HUMANIST STYLES.

ONIONSKIN PAPER: A VERY THIN YET STRONG PAPER (USUALLY 9#, LESS THAN HALF THE WEIGHT OF CONTEMPORARY

COPY PAPER) THAT WAS POPULAR FOR LETTERS WHEN POSTAL RATES WERE BASED ON WEIGHT.

OVERS: REMNANT SHEETS OF PAPER FROM THE MAKEREADY STAGE OF A PRESS RUN TO TEST INK DENSITY, COVERAGE, AND COLOR. THE FINAL COUNT OF A FINISHED PRESS RUN MAY BE IN EXCESS OF WHAT WAS ORDERED. SEE *PRESS PROOF*.

***PEINTER-GRAVEUR*:** AN ARTIST WHO WORKS IN AN ENGRAVING MEDIUM RATHFR THAN ONE WHO MAKES REPRODUCTIONS.

PHOTOENGRAVING: A PHOTOMECHANICAL ETCHING PROCESS THAT USES PHOTORESISTENT INTAGLIO PLATES. THERE ARE TWO KINDS OF PHOTOSENSITIVE INTAGLIO PLATES, BUT FOR THE MOST PART POSITIVE PHOTORESIST PLATES WITH NEGATIVE FILM ARE USED FOR COMMERCIAL ENGRAVING. MUCH AS ANALOG PHOTOGRAPHY IS DEVELOPED IN A DARKROOM, A POSITIVE PHOTORESIST PLATE IS EXPOSED TO A CONTROLLED SOURCE OF LIGHT, PLACED INTO A LIQUID DEVELOPER, AND THEN AGITATED IN A BATH TO REMOVE THE COATING ON THE PLATE WHERE IT WAS EXPOSED TO LIGHT THROUGH THE CLEAR PARTS OF THE FILM. EXPOSURE, DEVELOPING, AND A LIGHT WASHING RENDER THE AREAS OF THE PLATE WITHOUT COATING ACID-PERMEABLE. THE PLATE IS THEN PLACED INTO AN ACID BATH, AND THE ACID-PERMEABLE AREAS ARE ETCHED INTO THE METAL PLATE, INCISING THE ART INTO THE SURFACE OF THE METAL. EFFECTIVELY, THE ACID PERFORMS THE CUT. DETAILS MAY BE TOUCHED UP OR ENHANCED BY HAND WITH A GRAVER BEFORE THE PLATE IS SENT TO PRESS FOR THE PURPOSE OF

MAKING A SERIES OF PRINTS. ALMOST ALL CONTEMPORARY COMMERCIAL ENGRAVING IS DONE THIS WAY.

PLATE: THE MATRIX UPON WHICH AN ENGRAVING IS MADE. MOST COMMERCIAL ENGRAVING PLATES ARE 16 GAUGE, OR 0.06 INCHES IN THICKNESS. SEE ALSO *DIE*.

PMS (PANTONE MATCHING SYSTEM): A STANDARDIZED SYSTEM FOR COLOR SPECIFICATION AND MATCHING BETWEEN MULTIPLE MEDIA, SUCH AS PRINT, TEXTILES, AND DIGITAL.

PNEUMATIC ENGRAVING: THOUGH NOT A PROPER ENGRAVING TERM, THIS RELATIVELY RECENT METHOD OF ENGRAVING INVOLVES A SMALL HAND-HELD PNEUMATIC TOOL THAT IS MUCH LIKE A MINIATURE JACKHAMMER. A CONVENTIONAL GRAVER IS HELD IN A COMPRESSED AIR—DRIVEN DEVICE THAT DRIVES THE GRAVER FORWARD IN THE DIRECTION GUIDED BY THE HAND OF THE ENGRAVER.

PRESS PROOF: A TEST PRINT. AN ENGRAVED PROOF IS OFTEN MADE WITHOUT THE USE OF A COUNTER AND IS THE LAST STEP BEFORE PRODUCTION OF AN EDITION OR SET OF STATIONERY WHEN CHANGES OR CORRECTIONS CAN BE MADE TO THE ENGRAVED PLATE OR DIE.

PRINTMAKING: THE PROCESS OF MAKING MULTIPLE PRINTS FROM A SINGLE MATRIX. GENERALLY, THE TERM IS USED IN A FINE ART RATHER THAN COMMERCIAL CONTEXT.

PRINT JOBBER: ALSO CALLED JOBBING PRINTER OR JOBBING SHOP, THESE ESTABLISHMENTS ARE ENGAGED IN WHOLESALE PRINTING, SELLING PRINTING SERVICES TO OTHER PRINTERS WHO, IN TURN, SELL (RETAIL) TO THE GENERAL PUBLIC.

PUNCHCUTTER: ONE WHO CUTS TYPOGRAPHIC CHARACTERS INTO PUNCHES, THE ORIGINAL MASTER FROM WHICH LETTERPRESS TYPES ARE CAST. MANY PUNCHCUTTERS WERE ALSO TYPE DESIGNERS.

RAM: SEE *FORCE*.

SOCIAL STATIONERY: A VARIETY OF PAPER PRODUCTS USED FOR PERSONAL CORRESPONDENCE. SEE ALSO *LETTER PAPERS* AND *SOCIETY PAPERS*.

SOCIETY PAPERS: SEE *SOCIAL STATIONERY*.

SPOT COLOR PRINTING: PRINTING PROCESS IN WHICH INDIVIDUAL COLORS ARE PRINTED AS SOLID SHAPES (TYPE, IMAGE, OR HALFTONE) ONE AT A TIME. SPOT COLORS ARE USUALLY DESIGNATED AS PMS (SEE *PANTONE MATCHING SYSTEM*). THIS IS OPPOSED TO PROCESS OR FOUR-COLOR PRINTING, IN WHICH AN IMAGE IS MADE UP OF AN OVERALL PATTERN OF DOTS PRINTED IN FOUR LAYERS, ONE EACH OF CMYK (CYAN, MAGENTA, YELLOW, BLACK).

STEEL ENGRAVING: INVENTED IN THE EARLY TWENTIETH CENTURY AS A MORE DURABLE ALTERNATIVE TO USING COPPER PLATES. SEE ALSO *COPPERPLATE ENGRAVING*.

STOCK: PAPER, BOARD, OR ENVELOPES.

SUBSTRATE: THE SUBSTANCE, OR SURFACE, UPON WHICH AN IMAGE IS TO BE PRINTED, SUCH AS PAPER.

TERMINAL: WHEN ENGRAVING LETTERS, A TERMINAL IS WHERE THE BURIN, OR GRAVER, ENTERS AND EXITS A CUT.

THERMOGRAPHY: THIS PRINTING TECHNIQUE WAS DEVELOPED TO REPLICATE THE LOOK OF ENGRAVING. THERMOGRAPHY RELIES ON HEAT TO CREATE RAISED IMAGERY ON PAPER. IT IS LESS EXPENSIVE THAN ENGRAVING BUT NOT AS REFINED.

VISITING CARD: SEE *CALLING CARD.*

WHITE-LINE WOOD ENGRAVING: SEE *WOOD ENGRAVING.*

WOODCUT: THE OLDEST PRINTMAKING METHOD KNOWN, RESULTING IN A RELIEF PRINT. A DESIGN IS DRAWN ONTO THE LONG-GRAIN OF A PIECE OF WOOD, AND THE EXTRANEOUS AREAS ARE CUT AWAY WITH A SHARP TOOL. THE REMAINING RELIEF IS INKED, AND PAPER AND PRESSURE ARE APPLIED TO PRODUCE A PRINT.

WOOD ENGRAVING, OR WHITE-LINE WOOD ENGRAVING: WOODCUTS CREATED ON END-GRAIN WOOD AS OPPOSED TO THE SOFTER LONG-GRAIN WOOD, POPULARIZED BY THOMAS BEWICK (1753–1828), A GREAT NATURALIST WHO WAS TRAINED AS A METAL ENGRAVER. USING TRADITIONAL ENGRAVING TOOLS, ALL WHITE AREAS ARE METICULOUSLY CARVED AWAY, WITH THE HIGH, REMAINING SURFACES RECEIVING THE INK, PRODUCING A MUCH MORE DETAILED AND REFINED RELIEF PRINT THAN WOOD BLOCK PRINTING.

NOTES

Introduction

1 For more on this technique, see Bamber Gascoigne, *How to Identify Prints: A Complete Guide to Manual and Mechanical Processes from Woodcut to Ink-jet* (New York: Thames and Hudson, 1986), 5 a. b.

2 Political and social satire was also produced using lithography.

3 English printmaker and satirist William Hogarth (1697–1764) painted and engraved serial editions of *A Harlot's Progress* and *A Rake's Progress*, each of which illustrates a downward journey into debauchery and ruin.

4 In 1770, shortly after the Boston Massacre, in which British soldiers fired upon and killed a street mob protesting the British troops' visible presence in the city, Paul Revere (1735–1818) scooped fellow engravers by publishing his account of the deadly scuffle and selling out the edition of his print *The Bloody Massacre Perpetrated in King Street* before his competition. Revere, most famous for his "midnight ride," was a silversmith turned political activist and copperplate engraver during the American Revolution.

5 Another virtue of satiric and illustrative prints is that captions were often superfluous, so anyone, including the illiterate, could benefit from the ribald humor or irony. Advances in the production of cheap paper and printing around 1870 made it possible for more people to learn to read and write, but before then, reading primers, copy books, and writing utensils were too expensive for anyone but the rich.

6 Perhaps the most significant technical advances in commercial engraving in the last one hundred years have been the PERI-Etch system (discussed in the timeline), the development and adoption of water-based ink, and automatic inking, wiping, and paper feeding. The basic principles of either cutting or etching on metal and applying paper and pressure remain the same.

Timeline

1 Several people were very close to solving the challenges of using movable type at about the same time as Gutenberg, and movable type had been used in China and Korea long before Europeans began their quest at perfecting it as a practical printing method. This technology is of revolutionary importance to the history of printing, reading, writing, mass media, and intellectual literacy, because it allowed manuscripts to be reproduced more efficiently, in quantity, and much faster than the ancient practice of copying text by hand with a quill pen (or brush) one letter at a time.

2 It is speculated that one of the two or both printers may have worked for Johann Fust (ca. 1400–1466), one of Gutenberg's lenders and the person who subsequently took over Gutenberg's business when he defaulted on his loans.

3 "Until 15 years ago, the letterheads of large firms across the country looked nearly identical: the firm name was centered at the top of the page, engraved in black ink....Variation was limited to the election of one of a narrow range of engraver's type fonts that had changed little from those used by law firms in the 19th century." According to the survey, 83 percent of law firm letterhead was engraved. By 2003 it was down to 79 percent. See Burkey Belser and George Kell, "Innovation vs. Tradition as Seen in 100 Law Firm Letterheads," and Elonide C. Semmes, "Letter of the Law, Lessons from Law Firm Letterhead," Greenfield/Belser, Ltd., Washington, DC, 1994 and 2003, http://www.greenfieldbelser.com/articles/innovation-vs-tradition-as-seen-in-100-law-firm-letterheads and http://www.greenfieldbelser.com/articles/letter-of-the-law-lessons-from-law-firm-letterhead (accessed Nov. 11, 2011). Letterhead samples from one hundred of the nation's largest law firms were collected and analyzed for this survey.

4 "History," BurdgeCooper, http://www.burdgecooper.com/who-we-are/history (accessed Oct. 23, 2011).

Chapter One

1 The earliest engravings were used for religious purposes and for gambling, in the form of playing cards.
2 A print jobber, or jobbing shop, prints and sells wholesale to other printers, who offer their services to the public. Generally, a print jobber does not sell retail or directly to the public.
3 Jane Austen, in a letter to her sister, Cassandra. See Penelope Hughes-Hallett, ed., *Jane Austen: My Dear Cassandra, The Illustrated Letters* (New York: Collins & Brown Limited, 1990).

Chapter Two

1 Dard Hunter, *Papermaking: The History and Technique of an Ancient Craft* (New York: Dover Publications, 1978), 60.
2 Silvie Turner, *The Book of Fine Paper* (New York: Thames and Hudson, 1998), 14.
3 Aurora Cuito, ed., *Store Window Design* (New York, teNeues Publishing, 2005), 5.
4 Deborah Davis, *Strapless: John Singer Sargent and the Fall of Madame X* (New York: Jeremy P. Tarcher, 2004), 29.
5 Nancy A. Pope, "Envelopes in the Machine Age," *EnRoute* 6, no. 2 (April–June 1997), National Postal Museum, http://www.postalmuseum.si.edu/resources/6a2o_envelopes.html (accessed Dec. 30, 2010).
6 Maurice Rickards, *The Encyclopedia of Ephemera: A Guide to the Fragmentary Documents of Everyday Life for the Collector, Curator, and Historian* (New York: Routledge, 2000), 207.
7 Ibid., 208.
8 Pope, "Envelopes in the Machine Age." 9 Maynard H. Benjamin, *The History of Envelopes* (Envelope Manufacturers Association and EMA Foundation for Paper-Based Communications, 2002), 5.
10 From 2007 to 2011 the United States Postal Service laid off 110,000 employees and cut budgets by twelve billion dollars; U.S Senator John McCain, Arizona, http://www.mccain.senate.gov/public/index.

Chapter Three

1 John H. Young, *A Guide to the Manners, Etiquette, and Deportment of the Most Refined Society* (New York: Lyons Press, 2001), 75, originally published in 1879 by W. C. King & Co., Springfield, MA, as *Our Deportment, or the Manners, Conduct and Dress of the Most Refined Society; Including Forms for Letters, Invitations, Etc., Etc., Also Valuable Suggestions on Home Culture and Training.*
2 While the telephone was invented around the same time as the automobile, it was not used as a social mechanism until the twentieth century.
3 Rickards, *The Encyclopedia of Ephemera*, 351.
4 Duane Noriyuki, "Calling on the Past," *Los Angeles Times*, April 23, 2000, E2; and Young, *A Guide to the Manners*, 78.
5 Jessica Helfand, *Scrapbooks: An American History* (New Haven, CT: Yale University Press, 2008), 81.
6 Lesley M. M. Blume, "Leaving the Right Impression," *Wall Street Journal*, April 16, 2011, http://online.wsj.com/article/SB1000142405274870450310457625111104836958 4.html (accessed April 17, 2011).
7 Steven L. Feinberg, ed. *Crane's Blue Book of Stationery: The Styles and Etiquette of Letters, Notes, and Invitations* (New York: Doubleday, 1989), 206.
8 Commercial paper specification can be daunting because the descriptions for the heaviness or thickness of a paper are different for different uses. Paper specified for stationery (called "writing") is sold in different sizes than "text" (the paper used for printed books and brochures). The latter is also called "offset" because offset lithography was once the prevailing kind of commercial printing. "Cover" is the heaviest (such as card stock). A 24# writing

paper may be the same thickness as a 60# text, or offset, sheet. While we buy paper by weight, it is also specified by caliper, which measures a paper's thickness in one-thousandth-of-an-inch increments.

9 Excerpt, diagram, and photograph from interview of the author by Tom Biederbeck, Mohawk Fine Paper, in "A new morning for mourning stationery?" *Felt & Wire*, Aug. 8, 2010, http://www.feltandwire.com/2010/08/11/a-new-morning-for-mourning-stationery (accessed Feb. 9, 2011).

Chapter Five

1 "Ladies Gossip," [Dunedin, New Zealand] *Otago Witness* 1,957 (May 23, 1889): 33, Papers Past, National Library of New Zealand, http://paperspast.natlib.govt.nz/cgi-bin/paperspast?a=d&d=OW18890523.2.138&l=mi&e=-------10--1----2-- (accessed Oct. 24, 2011).

2 Kristen Regina, head of research collections, Hillwood Estate, Museum & Gardens, Washington, DC, telephone interview by the author and subsequent e-mail correspondence, June 6, 2011.

3 John M. Bergling's *Heraldic Designs for Artists and Craftspeople*, first published in 1913, and other books and websites attest to this long-standing American predilection.

4 Packets of these were sold cheaply (seventy-two mixed specimens for a whole shilling, thirty-six for a sixpence), indicating that they probably were proffered without authorization from the famous person, or royal, for whom it was created; see Rickards, *The Encyclopedia of Ephemera*, 112.

Chapter Six

1 See, for example, "Engraving," The Engraver's Cafe, http://www.engraverscafe.com (accessed Sept. 5, 2011). Though intended for gun and decorative knife engraving, this website of master hand-engraver Sam Alfano is a good resource.

2 Apprentice time for mastering engraving with conventional tools takes anywhere from six to ten years. In general, engraving with a graver or burin is not offered as a major in college degree programs in the United States but is often integrated in the printmaking departments of many colleges and universities under the subject of intaglio printing. There are still a few trade schools that teach engraving, primarily for the jewelry and gunsmithing trades. One of the oldest continuously running trade schools in the country is Gem City College in Quincy, Illinois, which trains students in watchmaking, engraving, and other specialty vocations.

3 Most commercial engraving today is actually etched.

4 In general, there are two ways to think about accomplishing your ideal engraving. One approach is to have your design complete and ready to go before contacting the engraver, and the second is to make a sketch of what you propose and then create your finished artwork according to the advice from the engraver you intend to commission. With a comprehensive and well-conceived sketch in hand, there should be room for modification and improvement based on information you discuss, letting the engraver's expertise be part of the process.

5 The Cronite Company manufactures, sells, and services the Masterplate system and the pantograph used with it, the Zero Engraving Machine.

6 The GRS pneumatic system was invented by Donald A. Glaser, founder of the Glendo Corporation of Emporia, Kansas. Glendo has endowed a professorship at Emporia State University, Emporia, Kansas, which offers "the world's only" BFA degree in engraving arts, a four-year program. Glendo's GRS Training Center provides a vocational program that is much shorter in duration than the BFA program at Emporia State; the GRS tools are typically mastered in approximately four months. See "About Glendo," Glendo Corporation, http://www.glendo.com/about (accessed July 3, 2011).

7 "Interview with Koichi Yamamoto" McClain's Printmaking Supplies, Aug. 9, 2010, http://imcclains.com/newsletter/?p=505 (accessed July 3, 2011).

8 Artwork drawn in graphite pencil on tracing paper can be transferred to another substrate by scribbling a layer of graphite on the back of the drawing; placing this side on the plate or die in the position at which the engraving will be cut; and firmly tracing the original drawing on the front with a very sharp and hard pencil (perhaps H, 2 or 4H in hardness). The pressure transfers the graphite onto the metal.

9 In the history of cartography, there is a legacy of punching up mistakes and making revisions, with maps altered multiples times over the course of their use. See the discussion of this topic by Tony Campbell, former map librarian, British Library, London, "Understanding Engraved Maps," Map History, http://www.maphistory.info/understanding.html#change (accessed Dec. 1, 2010).

10 A third kind of press—the screw press—was once used for proofing dies. It functions similarly to a duck or old-fashioned laundry press. The demonstration in figure 45 was done on such a press.

11 Intaglio ink traditionally has been varnish based, but water-based inks have been used in commercial engraving for several decades now. Varnish-based inks require toxic high-VOC solvents and are destructive to the environment and hazardous to human health.

12 For example, if the engraved portion and the border of a card need to be the same color, it is advisable to color proof both. Most vendors are able to facilitate some form of proofing before a job is run. As time, geographic location, and budget allow, I urge all designers to proof elements, in person if possible, prior to approving production.

13 Metallic ink pigment particles appear larger than nonmetallic particles, making fine detail difficult to accomplish. Metallic inks can also bleed or show through to the back of some papers. It is recommended to do a "bump," a second, dry pass through the press without ink, which burnishes the surface and flattens it out, making it uniform and more reflective.

14 These days, in most commercial presses for engraved stationery, the plates are inked and wiped automatically. Automatic inking and wiping speed up the process enormously, making it much more cost effective than when each function is performed by hand.

15 Colloquially, in south Louisiana the term is used to mean "a little something extra."

Appendix B

1 JMC Engraver and Feldman Engraver can be downloaded for free from www.fonts.com/browse/promotions/the-complete-engraver. JMC Engraver and Feldman Engraver are not the first engraver's fonts to be made popularly available. Sackers, part of the ATSackers family of display fonts by Monotype Imaging, was based on photocomposition styles developed by Compugraphic Corporation in the early 1970s for thermographic printing. These styles seem to have been derived from an earlier photocomposition system, Hadego, invented by H. J. A. de Goeij in the Netherlands in the 1940s. Interestingly, Hadego was purchased by American Type Foundry, which has a long history of marketing lettering styles that cater to the social stationery industry.

BIBLIOGRAPHY

Alexander, Thomas J. *The Queen's Own: Stamps That Changed the World.* Washington, DC: Smithsonian Institution National Postal Museum, 2004.

Becker, David P. *The Practice of Letters: The Hofer Collection of Writing Manuals, 1514–1800.* Cambridge, MA: Harvard College Library, 1997.

Bergling, John M. *Art Alphabets and Lettering.* 1914. Reprint, Quincy, IL: Gem City College Press, 1995.

———. *Art Monograms and Lettering.* 1910. Reprint, Quincy, IL: Gem City College Press, 1992.

———. *Heraldic Designs for Artists and Craftspeople.* 1913. Reprint, Mineola, NY: Dover Publications, 1997.

———. *Heraldic Designs and Engravings Manual.* 1913. Reprint, Quincy, IL: Gem City College Press, 1994.

———. *Ornamental Designs and Illustrations.* 1913. Reprint, Quincy, IL: Gem City College Press, 1992.

Bickham, George. *The Universal Penman, Engraved by George Bickham, London, 1743.* Reprint, New York: Dover Publications, 1941.

Cirker, Hayward, and Blanche Cirker, eds. *Monograms and Alphabetic Devices.* New York: Dover Publications, 1970.

Drucker, Johanna, and Emily McVarish. *Graphic Design History: A Critical Guide.* Upper Saddle River, NJ: Pearson Prentice Hall, 2009.

Feinberg, Steven L. *Crane's Blue Book of Stationery: The Styles and Etiquette of Letters, Notes, and Invitations.* New York: Doubleday, 1989.

Fox-Davies, Arthur Charles. *Heraldry: A Pictorial Archive for Artists and Designers.* New York: Dover Publications, 1991.

Gascoigne, Bamber. *How to Identify Prints: A Complete Guide to Manual and Mechanical Processes from Woodcut to Ink-jet.* New York: Thames and Hudson, 1986.

Hind, Arthur M. *A History of Engraving & Etching, from 15th Century to the Year 1914.* 1923. Reprint, New York: Dover Publications, 1963.

Hunter, Dard. *Papermaking: The History and Technique of an Ancient Craft.* 1947. Reprint, New York: Dover Publications, 1978.

Kane, John. *A Type Primer.* Upper Saddle River, NJ: Prentice Hall, 2003.

Meggs, Philip B., and Alston W. Purvis. *Megg's History of Graphic Design.* 4th ed. New York: Wiley, 2005.

Melot, Michel, et al. *Prints: History of an Art.* New York: Skira/Rizzoli, 1985.

Meyer, Franz Sales. *Handbook of Ornament.* New York: Dover Publications, 1957.

Pope, Nancy A. "Envelopes in the Machine Age," *EnRoute* 6, no. 2, April–June 1997, http://www.postalmuseum.si.edu/resources/6a2o_envelopes.html (accessed Dec. 30, 2010).

Powers, William. *Hamlet's BlackBerry: A Practical Philosophy for Building a Good Life in the Digital Age.* New York: Harper Collins Publishers, 2010.

Rickards, Maurice. *The Encyclopedia of Ephemera: A Guide to the Fragmentary Documents of Everyday Life for the Collector, Curator, and Historian*. New York: Routledge, 2000.

Steffens, Robert N. *Engraved Stationery Handbook*. New York: Cronite Co., 1950.

Turbayne, A. A. *Monograms and Ciphers*. 1909. Reprint, New York: Dover Publications, 1968.

Turner, Silvie. *The Book of Fine Paper*. New York: Thames and Hudson, 1998.

Young, John H. *A Guide to the Manners, Etiquette, and Deportment of the Most Refined Society*. 1879. Reprint, New York: Lyons Press, 2001.

INDEX

GOOD-BYE.